Pousadas
of
Portugal

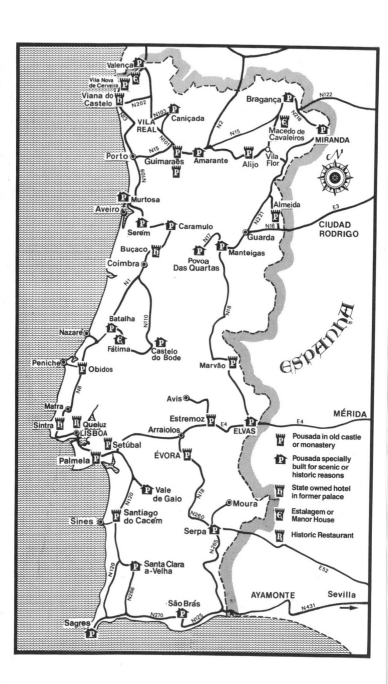

Grateful acknowledgment is made to Suzanne and João Carvalho-Maia, Quinta de Santo Domingos, Vila Flor, Portugal, and to our editor, Kenneth Hale-Wehmann.

CONTENTS

A fisherman perches precariously near the Pousada do Infante, Sagres.

INTRODUCTION

Market day in Barcelos, Roman gardens at Conímbriga, Manueline architecture, cork trees with orange trunks, broad avenues tiled in mosaics, brilliant cerulean *azulejos*, legends of virtuous thirteenth-century Queen Saint Isabel and torrid lovers Dom Pedro and Inês de Castro, the haunting presence of Prince Henry the Navigator—these are a few of the fascinations of Portugal.

How best to experience the charm of villages little changed for centuries, to visit awesome monuments of Portugal's illustrious past, to savor a different cuisine, to sample tantalizing wines? By touring the countryside and spending each night in the comfort of one of the state-owned pousadas.

In 1940, António de Oliveira Salazar, dictator of Portugal for over thirty years, inaugurated the network of pousadas, patterned after Spain's paradores. The country was badly in need of modern accommodations for tourists. Castles, monasteries, and mansions have been converted into pousadas. New buildings in contemporary and regional styles have been erected along coasts, in highlands and mountains, and near historic sites. Decor and furnishings correspond to each pousada's history and personality. The pousadas are state-owned and are managed by ENATUR, a national tourist agency.

Because of the relatively small size of most of the pousadas, the visitor has the opportunity to converse with personnel and fellow travelers from all over the world. Guests tend to gather in the lounges before and after meals, and a general camaraderie prevails.

In addition to the pousadas, three state-owned hotels, two privately owned hotels, two state-owned restaurants, five *estalagens* (privately owned inns; the singular is *estalagem*), and two manor houses are covered in this guide. The latter are part of a phenomenon whereby some Portuguese are opening their *solares* (mansions) to tourists, in the style of bed and breakfasts. The Portuguese National Tourist Office distributes a pamphlet listing such houses. But directions are so meager that only tourists with unlimited time can spend the necessary hours to locate them.

All pousadas are rated by the Ministry of Tourism as CH, C, and B, with CH being the highest ("ch" is a consonant in its own right in Portuguese). Hotels, *estalagens*, and manor houses receive a star rating from the ministry.

1986 Prices for a Double Room with Breakfast (in Escudos)

	RATING		
SEASON	B	C	CH
Low (Nov. 1–Dec. 20, Jan. 2–Feb. 6, Feb. 13–March 1)	3600	4900	6900
Medium (March–June 30 and Oct.)	5950	7750	9950
High (July–Sept., Dec. 21–Jan. 1, Feb. 7–12)	6850	8950	12,000

HOW TO USE THIS GUIDE

Descriptions of places to stay, eat, and visit are presented in rough geographical order following a circuit from Lisboa north along the coast to the Spanish border, then inland to Bragança and south along the Spanish border, west along the southern coast of Portugal—the Algarve—and back to Lisboa.

Two indexes and the table of contents provide the key to finding what you're looking for. If you want to know whether a certain city has a pousada, *estalagem,* or government hotel or restaurant, and where the establishment appears in this book, use the Index by Locale. If the name of the lodging or restaurant is known, but not its location, see the Index by Establishment.

Numerous maps help to pinpoint pousadas and plan your own routes. A map at the start of most write-ups shows which roads a particular establishment is on and near. These maps are not designed to replace road maps but are simply schematic drawings. Special symbols are used on these maps and on the map of the entire country to show various kinds of establishments:

🏰 denotes pousada in castle or monastery

🏰 denotes state-owned hotel in former palace

🏰 denotes pousada specially built for scenic or historic reasons

🏰 denotes estalagem

In the Recommended Itineraries section, each itinerary is accompanied by a map to show at a glance the general outline of the route.

Throughout this book, the abbreviation "km" is used for kilometers (a kilometer is .62 mile).

The reader will find historical, art-historical, and architectural terms frequently encountered in the Glossary.

RESERVATIONS

Portugal is becoming more and more popular with bargain-seeking Europeans and North Americans. Therefore reservations must be made well in advance of a proposed trip. Remember that there are three stages of enjoyment realized from a journey: the preliminary planning, the adventure itself, and the reliving of it for years afterward.

Reservations may be made by writing to individual pousadas. The mailing address is given in each pousada write-up (the number preceding town or province names in write-ups is a postal code). Include a personal check equal to one night's lodging (new price lists are available yearly from the Portuguese National Tourist Office). It has been our experience to find our uncashed check waiting for us. If you are traveling off season, secure the first night's accommodation beforehand, and then a member of the pousada staff will telephone ahead to arrange for subsequent nights. Rooms are held until 5 P.M. If you find you will be late—by even five minutes—telephone ahead.

Bookings may also be made by contacting ENATUR directly (phone 88 12 21 (Lisboa), telex 13609).

The following agencies can give you confirmation of a reservation within 24 hours of making it. Naturally the prices will be higher than if you traveled independently and made your own arrangements.

- Encore Tours, 1299 Kingsway, Vancouver, B.C., Canada V5V 3E2 (phone 604/879-4679)
- JM Sun Spree Vacations, 421 Eglinton Avenue West, #3, Toronto, Ontario, Canada M5N 1A4 (phone 416/440-0150, telex 06-217890) (deals with travel agents only)

Portuguese National Tourist Offices

- *1801 McGill College Avenue, #1150, Montreal, Quebec, Canada H3A 2N4*
- *548 Fifth Avenue, New York, NY 10036*

- Marketing Ahead, 433 Fifth Avenue, 6th Floor, New York, NY 10016 (phone 212/686-9213)
- Marsans International, 3325 Wilshire Boulevard, #508, Los Angeles, CA 90010, and 205 East 42d Street, #1514, New York, NY 10017

TOUR OPERATORS

If your time in Portugal is limited, you may want to take advantage of comprehensive tours offered by several tour companies. Your hotel clerk can give information about these. There are tours of Lisboa and also tours to Sintra, Mafra, Nazaré, and other places. Fly-drive do-it-yourself packages and guided tours featuring pousadas are offered by the following companies:

- Abreu Tours, 60 East 42d Street, New York, NY 10165 (phone 212/661-0555)
- Cavalcade Tours, 5 Penn Plaza, New York, NY 10001 (phone 212/695-6400)
- C Air Holidays, 733 Summer Street, Stamford, CT 06901 (phone 203/356-9033)
- Encore Tours, 1299 Kingsway, Vancouver, B.C., Canada V5V 3E2 (phone 604/879-4679)
- Extra Value Travel, 437 Madison Avenue, New York, NY 10022 (phone 212/750-8800)
- JM Sun Spree Vacations, 421 Eglinton Avenue West, #3, Toronto, Ontario, Canada M5N 1A4 (phone 416/440-0150; telex 06-217890). Deals with travel agents only.
- Maupintour, 900 Mass. Street, Lawrence, KS 66044 (phone 913/843-1211)
- Memo Tours, 310 Madison Avenue, New York, NY 10022 (phone 212/697-6868)
- Portuguese Tours, 321 Rahway Avenue, Elizabeth, NJ 07207 (phone 201/352-6112)
- Top Tours Int'l, 307 Fifth Avenue, New York, NY 10016 (phone 212/889-8390)

BORDER CROSSINGS

Portugal has land frontiers only with Spain. The locations and hours of opening for crossing points are given in the table Portuguese-Spanish Border Crossings. There are tourist offices at Caia, Galegos (Marvão), Valença do Minho, Vila Real de Santo António, and Vilar Formoso.

Portuguese-Spanish Border Crossings

Portugal	Spain	April–Oct.	Nov.–March
Caminha	LaGuardia	9 A.M.–6 P.M.	9 A.M.–6 P.M.
Valença do Minho	Tuy	7 A.M.–1 A.M.	8 A.M.–midnight
São Gregório	Puentes Barijas	7 A.M.–midnight	8 A.M.–9 P.M.
Portela do Homem	Lovios	7 A.M.–9 P.M.	closed
Vila Verde da Raia	Feces be Abajo	7 A.M.–midnight	8 A.M.–9 P.M.
Quintanilha	Alcañices	7 A.M.–midnight	8 A.M.–9 P.M.
Miranda do Douro	Torre Jamones	7 A.M.–midnight*	8 A.M.–9 P.M.*
Barca d'Alva	La Fregeneda	7 A.M.–midnight	8 A.M.–9 P.M.
Vilar Formoso	Fuentes de Oñoro	7 A.M.–midnight	8 A.M.–midnight
Segura	Piedras Albas	7 A.M.–midnight	8 A.M.–9 P.M.
Marvão	Valencia de Alcántara	7 A.M.–midnight	8 A.M.–9 P.M.
Caia	Caya	7 A.M.–midnight	8 A.M.–midnight
São Leonardo	Vila Nueva del Fresno	7 A.M.–midnight	8 A.M.–9 P.M.
Vila Verde de Ficalho	Rosal de la Frontera	7 A.M.–midnight	8 A.M.–9 P.M.
Vila Real de Santo António	Ayamonte	8 A.M.–midnight	8 A.M.–9 P.M.

*Closed Jan. 16–May 31.

AUTOMOBILES

The tour operators already listed can also arrange car rentals. Cars can be rented at the airport in Lisboa, but it is best to have made prior arrangements through your travel agent. For extended stays you may want to purchase a car to be delivered in Europe, then shipped home. (If you opt for this plan, make sure to order the car made to U.S. specifications.) Your travel agent can handle details for you, working with companies such as Europe-by-Car. They can also arrange a purchase-repurchase plan, in reality a long-term lease. The advantage to this plan is that you are assured of a new car. The disadvantage is that you must plan your itinerary around pick-up and drop-off cities.

Driving conditions have been changing—for the worse. Just a few years ago there was little traffic on highways and in smaller towns. Now Portugal has the highest accident rate in Europe, a statistic that makes defensive driving imperative. Noise pollution is caused by thousands of motor bikes without mufflers. The increased population in small towns is noticed when the motorist creeps through town; often villagers stand in the streets or overflow the sidewalks. Proceed with caution.

Traffic signs are international. Unless posted to the contrary, traffic on the right has priority. The speed limit in outlying areas is 60 kilometers per hour, on highways 90 kilometers per hour, and on freeways, called *autostradas*, 120 kilometers per hour. Should you be forced to pull over for any emergency, use of the caution triangle is mandatory. It is usually found in the trunk of a rental car. Although seat belts and an international drivers license are not mandatory at this writing, they probably will be in the near future.

Gas stations appear frequently but it is always wise not to run too low on fuel. Stations are open from 7 A.M. until midnight; some stay open 24 hours a day. The cost of gasoline is high by U.S. standards, but remember that distances are not great and cars get very high mileage per gallon or liter.

Count on averaging between 40 and 50 kilometers per hour on narrow winding roads and between 90 and 100 on straight stretches.

TRAINS

Extensive train travel through Portugal will appeal only to ardent enthusiasts. Exceptions are the expresses between Lisboa and Porto and during the summer between these two cities and the Algarve. These trains have bar and restaurant cars. Short jaunts from Lisboa to Sintra or Cascais, for example, are adequately comfortable. It is important to remember that you cannot board a Portuguese train without a previously purchased ticket. To do so brings a very high fine.

Wagons-lits (sleeper cars) are available on TER or Lusitania Express between Madrid and Lisboa and on the Sud Express from Paris.

AIRLINES

In 1944 the Portuguese government made plans for a national airline, Transportes Aereos Portugueses, or TAP Air Portugal. The first planes were in the air in 1946. Today TAP serves 24 countries, across four continents. Flights leave New York for Lisboa and Boston for Lisboa and the Azores.

TWA has regular service to and from Lisboa.

Out of Canada TAP and CP Air fly from Montreal to the Azores and Lisboa.

CULTURE

The Portuguese seem as fond of bullfights as the Spanish. One difference may lure reluctant tourists to a bullring in Portugal: The bull is not killed. However, as he is herded exhausted and subdued from the ring by frisky calves, one wonders how long the brave bull will live, now stripped of his raison d'etre. It is usually possible to take in a bullfight no matter what time of year you are in Portugal—if not in Lisboa, in small towns during their *festas*.

If you want to hear music typical of the country, ask the hotel clerk to recommend a *casa de fado*. The *fado*, a plaintive song recounting twists of fate, is sung by a man or woman accompanied by guitarists. *Casas de fado* serve dinner, snacks, and drinks. Performances begin any time after nine in the evening.

LANGUAGE

The centuries-old alliance between Portugal and England is a break for English-speaking tourists. In larger cities and towns there is usually someone on hand who speaks English. But in remote areas, this may not be true. You can try French and if that fails, have a go at Portuguese.

Though Portuguese and Spanish are both Romance languages and many words look similar, they sound quite different from one another. Try not to speak Spanish (even though it will probably be understood). Instead, blunder along and when unsure ask "Como se diz?" (How do you say?) or "Como se chama?" (What is it called?). Even the most meager, erroneous endeavor pleases the Portuguese, who instantly become willing teachers. So, plunge ahead and have fun.

There are now several Portuguese phrase books and pocket dictionaries on the market. Try to buy a tape to get some idea of pronunciation. Here are a few generalizations that may be helpful:

- Final *e* is barely pronounced. Instead, strongly stress the preceding consonant. For example, Amarante is ah-mah-RAHNT.
- *S* in the middle and at the end of a word has the "sh" sound. *Esta* is ESH-tah.
- *O* at the end of a word has the "oo" sound of "food." *Como esta?* is COH-moo ESH-tah?
- The dipthong *ão* is a nasal "ow" sound. *J* is pronounced like the "s" in "measure" or "treasure." For instance, João (John) is the "measure" "s" plus wow: zh-WOW.
- *Lh* and *nh* are liquid; that is, *lh* sounds like the middle of "million" and *nh* like the middle of "onion." *Vinho* (wine) is VEEN-yoo.
- *R* is trilled vigorously.
- *X* usually has the "sh" sound: *Mixta* is MEESH-tah.
- Unless marked with an accent, words ending in a vowel, *m*, *s*, or *ns* have stress on the next-to-last syllable. For example, *farmacia* is far-mah-SEE-ah. Words ending in all other consonants have stress on the last syllable. For example, *real* is ray-AL.

A few words and phrases you will use constantly:

Good morning: *bom dia*. *Bom* is pronounced nasally like the French *bon* (bon DEE-uh).
Good afternoon: *boa tarde* (BOH-ah TARD).
Good evening: *boa noite* (BOH-ah NOH-eet).
Yes: *sim* (seen).
No: *não* (nown).
Please: *por favor* (poor fah-VOOR).
Thank you: men say *obrigado* (oh-bree-GAH-doo) and women say *obrigada* (oh-bree-GAH-dah).
Excuse me: *desculpe* (des-COOL-pa).
Restroom: *lavabo* (la-VAH-boo).
Room: *quarto* (KWAR-too).
Where: *onde* (ohnd).
When: *quando* (KWAHN-doo).
How much: *quanto* (KWAHN-too).

Do you speak English?: *Fala ingles?* (FAH-lah een-GLAYSH?).

I don't understand: *Não compreendo* (now cohn-pree-EHN-doo).

How do you say?: *Como se diz?* (COH-moo se DEESH?).

What is it called?: *Como se chama?* (COH-moo se SHA-mah?).

Goodbye: *adeus* (a-DAY-oosh).

BUSINESS HOURS AND HOLIDAYS

As a rule, shops are open from 9 A.M. to 1 P.M. and 3 P.M. to 7 P.M. Monday through Friday. From January to November, shops close Saturdays at 1 P.M. In December, shops remain open on Saturdays until 7 P.M. Shopping centers are usually open daily from 10 A.M. to midnight.

Museums are closed on Mondays.

Holidays can be something of a let-down for the unsuspecting tourist who arrives ready to see sights and explore, only to find everything at a standstill. Portugal's national holidays are:

January 1
Shrove Tuesday (last day before Lent)
Good Friday
April 25
June 10 (death of Camões, Portugal's most famous poet)
Corpus Christi
August 15
October 5 (Proclamation of the Republic)
November 1
December 1 (Restoration of Independence)
December 8
December 25

Holidays honoring patron saints differ from town to town. In Lisboa, Saint Anthony is honored on June 13. Write to the Portuguese National Tourist Office for a complete, up-to-date list of regional festivals.

SHOPPING

The major reason for packing light is to have room for some of Portugal's wonderful products. But don't let unavailable space stop you. Simply buy an inexpensive bag and fill it to the brim with beautiful objects you will enjoy for years.

Portugal produces some of the most elegant crystal in the world: Atlantis, with 30 percent lead and at prices far less than the most well-known crystal. The company now has a retail store in Amoreiras Shopping Center in Lisboa near the Ritz Hotel. It's easiest to take a cab to this unusual, postmodern mall. Another Atlantis outlet is in Cascais, a short train ride from Lisboa. Gift stores in Albufeira and Almansil on the Algarve also sell Atlantis.

Arraiolos carpets have a long history. Eighteenth-century examples hang on walls of museums and grace floors of palaces. Today's *tapêtes* are so colorful and distinctive that they are a real lure to the shopper. They are found in stores in Lisboa, are on display and for sale at the pousada and museum in Evora, and may be purchased in several shops in the town of Arraiolos, 20 km north of Evora. Go behind the scenes to watch fingers fly, following designs and working cross-stitch in wool on a linen base.

In Vista Alegre south of Aveiro, visit the porcelain factory founded in 1824 and still operated by the same family, the Pinto Bastos. They produce fine china comparable to highly regarded European lines. Fabrica de Louça in Viana do Castelo turns out high-quality ceramics, handpainted with designs of ancient origin.

Village potters produce a wide variety of ceramic ware. Around Barcelos, many different versions of the cock are seen as well as yellow and red glazed goods. Shops in Caldas da Rainha sell plates embellished with crabs, lobsters, and oysters. Around Alcobaça, more traditional ware is decorated in tones of blue. Along Highway N-1 from Porto south are roadside stores displaying and selling countless ceramic items.

In shops along the coast are handsome textile products. Visit Sandra's in Viana do Castelo for fine embroideries. The old adage "where there are nets, there is lace" is borne out in fishing villages such as Valença do Minho, Caminha, Póvoa de Varzim, Vila do Conde, Peniche, Setúbal, and Lagos on the Algarve. In these same areas, shops not only sell lace but the popular "fishermen's" sweaters. Guimarães is noted for bedspreads and drapes woven in a linenlike fabric and bordered with brilliant, distinctive patterns.

TIPPING

Although service is included in almost all bills, it is correct to leave additional escudos. TAP airline spells it out in their brochure "Travel Tips."

Porter	30–50 escudos per bag
Housekeeper	30 escudos per service
Doorman	20 escudos for calling a cab
Taxi driver	10 percent of the meter (fares are so reasonable that we usually tip 15 percent)
Waiters	50–100 escudos or 10 percent of bill
Barber	10 percent of bill
Hairdresser	10 percent of bill (15–20 percent if you're especially pleased with the results and the low bill)

Our modus operandi is to leave a tip of 10 percent of a pousada, *estalagem,* or hotel bill "for all employees"—more if telephone calls have been made for you. Tips are put into a common fund and shared by all employees. With the exception of the porter who carries luggage in and out and is tipped on the spot, and leaving loose change under the plate at mealtime, the "lump sum" method alleviates the constant doling out of escudos.

PHARMACIES

Every town has a *farmacia* and most pharmacists speak some English. To be on the safe side, take a phrase book that lists common ailments. Pharmacists are skilled in first aid. By law, one pharmacy in each area must be open 24 hours per day. Its location is posted in all neighboring pharmacies.

Visitors are amazed at seeing medicine that requires a prescription at home being sold over the counter—at much lower prices—in Portugal. The usual drugstore items such as aspirin, toothpaste, shaving cream, and shampoo are on sale in the pharmacies.

CLOTHING

Planning and packing a wardrobe is not a chore because Portugal enjoys such a mild climate year round. Take an all-purpose coat and a couple of light sweaters. Pantsuits are worn by women everywhere. Men will not feel uncomfortable without a tie at mealtime in pousada dining rooms. Shoes should be your number one consideration, for most walking surfaces are tessellated— of unevenly cut stones with few rounded edges. The tourist is in awe of young Portuguese women who trip along in wooden clogs, high-heeled boots and shoes, or bare feet.

Self-service laundromats in the North American style have not yet appeared in Portugal, although cities of some size and resorts along the Algarve have laundries where you can leave your clothing to be washed and folded. This is fine if you are in one place for more than a day. If not, plan on doing the laundry chore yourself. Take several plastic coat hangers, two or three inflatable hangers, and plastic and wooden clothespins to secure socks and the like to hangers. Plastic bags meant for food storage are handy for stowing soiled or not-yet-dry clothes. Water is so soft in Portugal that not much soap is needed. Buying soap becomes a shopping adventure as you try to discover which store sells this necessity. Tuck a bar of Lava soap in your luggage. It works wonders for removing stains.

MONEY MATTERS

Portugal's monetary unit is the escudo; one escudo is written "1$." There are 100 centavos to one escudo. Coin denominations are 25$, 10$, 5$, 2$50 (two escudos, 50 centavos), 1$, and $50 (50 centavos). Paper money comes in denominations of 5.000$ (5,000—the comma in thousands is written as a period), 1.000$, 500$, 100$, 50$, and 20$.

The most common credit cards are accepted throughout Portugal. If you carry credit cards, it is a good idea to have two—one for obtaining cash (Visa or American Express) and one for daily expenses. We found Barclay's banks willing to give us escudos on our credit card. This system minimizes the amount of travelers checks needed, easing the anxiety of having them stolen or lost. However, take care not to run too low on your cash reserve.

Before leaving home, buy just enough escudos to get through a couple of days until you can get to a bank, because exchange rates are better in Portugal. Normal banking hours are 9:30 A.M. to noon and 2 to 4 P.M. weekdays; banks are closed Saturdays and Sundays. Frontier, airport, and hotel money exchanges offer extended hours.

TIPS ON PHOTOGRAPHY

Camera enthusiasts will revel in the possibilities in Portugal. For the best candid shots, travel off the beaten track. It has been our experience that rural inhabitants no longer shy from cameras but are quite willing to pose for their picture.

For rich scenic shots, shoot early in the morning, late in the afternoon, and at sunset.

Despite claims that airport security checks are not harmful to film, we recommend that you either request hand inspection of your camera gear or carry all film in lead-laminated bags available at photographic stores. This is especially important if you are carrying some of the newer high-speed films.

The price of film in Portugal is not as high as it has been in the past, but it is still higher than in North America, so try to purchase enough ahead of time to last through your trip.

FOOD

Breakfast, *pequeno almoço,* is included in the price of a room, and consists of freshly baked crusty rolls, butter, jam, and coffee. If you are hardy and have a cast-iron stomach, you may order your coffee *simples,* black. Otherwise you will get it *com leite,* with hot milk. In addition to juice or fruit (which may cost extra), you may order bacon and eggs, but they probably won't taste the same as you're used to. Best to follow Portuguese breakfast customs.

Lunch, *almoço,* is the main meal of the day for many Portuguese, and is served between 1 and 3 P.M. The menu, *ementa,* may list as many as four courses: soup, fish, meat, and dessert. But you may order items a la carte or simply a tossed salad, *salada mixta*.

Dinner, *jantar*, is served from 7:30 to 9 P.M., although a few pousadas don't open the doors until 8.

Portuguese dishes, flavored with garlic and herbs, are very tasty. Soup always appears on the menu. *Caldo verde* is the universal favorite. With mashed potatoes as a base, bits of pork or sausage are added along with shredded *couve galega*, Galician cabbage. *Couve* is used in salads and often is the main vegetable. Leaves of this unique plant are plucked from the base as needed, leaving a spindly stalk sometimes reaching a height of six feet. It is seen in every garden patch and even among blooming flowers. *Sopa de coentros*, garlic soup made with coriander, olive oil, and garlic bread, is topped with a poached egg. If you don't go for an egg floating on your *sopa*, specify *sem ovo*, without egg. *Gaspacho*, a refreshing soup of chopped tomatoes, cucumbers, and onions, garnished with croutons, is very similar to Spain's version, with an added ingredient: bits of ham or sausage.

Fish is the primary food and it is of infinite variety. *Bacalhau*, cod, seems to be the staff of life; rarely is there a menu not offering cod in one form or another. The average Portuguese consumes 100 pounds of cod per year, a good indication of the importance of a large fishing fleet that for centuries has delivered cod from as far away as Greenland and Newfoundland. Sardines and tuna are fished from closer waters. Europe imports the greatest percentage of cannery products. Salmon, sole, sea bass, turbot, bream, hake, and swordfish are other deep-sea fish. Smoked swordfish is a popular appetizer. Shellfish include lobster, oysters, mussels, and clams. Eel, squid, octopus, and lamprey are other Iberian fish to be tried by the intrepid tourist. Sardines are grilled on street-side braziers and make tasty snacks. Fish stew, *caldeirada*, can be counted on as a delicious and hearty dish. Clams and pork in a savory wine sauce combine to make a very tempting entree.

Pork appears in many guises. *Leitão assado*, roast suckling pig, is the piece de resistance of Portuguese meats. Various parts of the hog are used to flavor stews and other dishes. *Presunto* is smoked ham, *salsicha* is fresh pork sausage, and *chouriço* is smoked, spiced sausage.

Chanfana is a favorite native dish to look for. It is a goat or mutton stew baked in red wine in an earthenware bowl in a bread oven.

Poultry and game are found on daily menus, with chicken, turkey, rabbit, duck, and partridge being the principal entrees.

Vegetables are always fresh; when cooked, they are pleasantly seasoned with olive oil, garlic, or bits of ham.

Dessert choices are *fruta* (fruit) or a *doce* (sweet). Portuguese *sobremesas* are as rich and luscious as they look and may be selected from the pastry cart. *Flan,* a custard with caramel topping, is a reliable standby.

Special mention must be made of Portuguese bread, *pão.* It is always crusty on the outside, soft inside, aromatic, addictive, and destined to put pounds on the willing visitor.

WINE

In the past, port has been synonymous with Portugal's wine. But in the last decade or two, table wines have constituted a large part of the country's wine exports, France being the major importer of both port and table wines. Sampling Portugal's wines can become a challenge for the palate and a hobby for the label collector.

There are nine demarcated wine zones in the country set up to assure high standards of wine production. In the north, from the Minho River south to the lower Douro River is the Vinho Verde zone. White and red *vinhos verdes* are produced. These "green wines" are consumed unaged and have a fresh natural effervescence.

The Port zone lies along the upper Douro River valley. Here grapes are crushed mechanically and the must ferments in giant vats until the desired level of sweetness is reached. At that time brandy is added to stop further fermentation and to retain the sweetness. The next step is the transference of the wine into casks for removal to wine vaults in Vila Nova de Gaia, across the river from Porto. There it is stored in large wooden vats for about two years. If tasters deem the wine fine enough to be declared "vintage" (this happens about every five years), it is bottled and permitted to age for 15 years or more. We found chilled white port, *porto branco,* a refreshing, satisfying apéritif.

In the zone around Vila Real, Mateus rosé, popular both in Europe and the U.S., had its beginning. Mateus made from red grapes with white pulp is a sweet, blended, artificially bubbly wine suitable to accompany any entree.

Nowadays wine is shipped from all parts of the country to company headquarters, 2 km outside Vila Real.

In the north-central Dão zone, grapes growing on rocky hillsides yield a full-bodied red rather like a burgundy and a pleasing white.

The Bairrada district, southwest of the Dão, produces a good red wine and naturally sparkling *espumantes,* both bruts (*brutos*) and dries (*secos*). A red *espumante* is an excellent choice with *leitão assado* (roast suckling pig) in the area near Mealhada.

The remaining demarcated regions are smaller in scope, due mainly to population encroachment. A smooth red and a fresh white are produced from sandy soil in Colares, near Sintra. Bucelas's dry whites are made from grapes growing along the Trancão River northeast of Colares. From the Carcavelos zone south of Colares comes a fruity dessert wine. Another popular dessert wine is *moscatel,* a fortified blend of black and white grapes grown on slopes of the Serra da Arrábida in the Setúbal zone. Also in this zone is the home of Lancers, an international favorite from the Fonseca winery in Azeitão.

The ninth demarcated area is found on the Algarve around Lagos and Lagoa, where both red and white wines are produced.

In general, if you are uncertain what wine to order at mealtime, a wise choice would be *vinho do casa,* the house wine, sure to be a good regional wine.

Portuguese toasts to try include "à sua saúde" (one person to another) and "à vossa saúde" (one person to a group), both meaning to your health, and "à nossa saúde," meaning to our health. But our favorite says it all: "à nossa," to us.

GEOGRAPHY AND CLIMATE

Forming one-fifth of the Iberian peninsula, Portugal is roughly the shape of a rectangle, 350 miles long north-south and between 70 and 140 miles wide east-west. In proportion to its area, Portugal's coastline is three times greater than the European average.

Three mighty rivers that rise in Spain—the Guadiana, Douro, and Tejo (Duero and Tajo in Spanish)—continue their flow through Portugal.

Although essentially a homogeneous land (that is, there are no nationalistic groups like those of Cataluña and Vascongadas in Spain), Portugal does have traditional regions that serve as convenient guideposts for discussing and touring the country. From south to north the regions are the Algarve, Alentejo, Estremadura, Beira, Trás-os-Montes, and the Minho. These were partly subdivided into provinces in 1936.

The Algarve is separated from the Alentejo by low mountain ranges gradually sloping to a coastal plain. Here warm climate and fertile soil produce almonds, figs, oranges, olives, vegetables, flowers, some grapes, and wheat. Canneries employ citizens of small fishing communities along the Mediterranean Sea. Faro is the district capital of the Algarve.

While most of the Alentejo is bleak in color, it is restful to the eye, as vast grain fields are broken by occasional clumps of cork oaks. There are few isolated dwellings in this land of very hot summers. Instead, inhabitants congregate in small villages, perhaps to escape the loneliness of the Alentejo. This is the area of *latifundios*, large estates whose owners over the centuries have exploited the peasant population, similar to the situation in Spain's Extremadura and Andalucia. Most of the Communist movements in Portugal today have sprouted from the Alentejo's working class. Portalegre and Evora are the district capitals of Alto Alentejo (upper sector) while Beja reigns in Baixo Alentejo (lower sector).

Estremadura begins west of the Tejo estuary. The region is bounded by Lisboa, Setúbal, and the Serra da Arrábida on the south, the Serra de Sintra on the west, and coastal Nazaré on the north. Lisboa and Setúbal are district capitals of Estremadura province, and Santarém is the capital of Ribatejo, famous for bull breeding.

In Beira, Portugal's central region, there are three provinces. Beira Baixa is bordered on the south by the Alentejo, on the west by Ribatejo and Beira Litoral, and on the north by Beira Alta. Castelo Branco is the district capital.

Beira Litoral is separated by the Mondego River into two distinct coastal areas, one around Aveiro where marshes and lagoons are fed by the Vouga River, the other a rambling pine forest originally conceived and planted by King Dinis to secure sand dunes. Inland, the Litoral has some of Portugal's most beautiful and interesting countryside ranging along the Mondego, Dão, and Zêzere river valleys. Aveiro, Coimbra, and Leiria are district capitals of the Litoral.

Beira Alta is a geographic extension of Spain's Meseta, or central plateau, although physical differences are apparent on the descent from Guarda into the valley of the Mondego, which flows southwest along the country's highest mountain range, Serra da Estrêla, whose peaks reach altitudes of 6500 feet. Guarda and Viseu are the district capitals.

Trás-os-Montes (meaning across the mountains) has two contrasting climate areas. In *Terra Fria,* rye and chestnuts are grown despite long, cold winters. *Terra Quente*'s warmer weather encourages prolific terraced vineyards and olive groves nurtured by tributaries of the Douro: the Tâmega, Corgo, Tua, and Sabor rivers. The Serras de Barrosa, da Cabriera, and do Marão had geographically isolated Trás-os-Montes from the rest of Portugal until about 30 years ago, when roads were constructed linking countless hillside villages. An indication of this isolation is that as late as 1970, one in four Trás-os-Montes citizens was illiterate. Bragança is the northern district capital and Vila Real the southern.

Portugal's northern seaboard region takes its name from its natural border with Spain, the Minho River. The Minho's inhabitants, *minhotos,* have much in common with Spain's Galicians, *gallegos.* Green lush land receives prodigious rainfall, allowing intensive cultivation and thick pine groves. Similar customs and dialects prevail in the two regions. *Espigueiros,* granite family granaries, are similar to Galicia's *horreos.* Ponderous, squeaking carts are pulled along by handsome *gado barrosão* (oxen joined by decorative *cangas,* yokes). This is the land of *minifundios,* where tiny plots of land yield vines coaxed along granite posts and trellises and up trunks of trees. The delicious *vinho verde* (light, slightly bubbly wine) is produced in this region. Braga and Viana do Castelo are capitals of the Minho.

Portugal ranks first in world-wide cork production, sixth in wine and olive oil. It is one of the world's largest producers of tungsten. Extensive marble quarries bring additional income from home and foreign markets.

SUGGESTED READING

The Lusiads, by Luiz Vaz de Camões, is considered the national epic poem of Portugal, written in the sixteenth century. Penguin Books publishes a translation by William C. Atkinson.

The Wines of Portugal, by Jan Read, is a comprehensive study of the history and all current facets of wine production (Faber and Faber, 1982).

The Winding Stair, by Jane Aiken Hodge, is a mystery with historic undertones set in the time when the cult of Sebastianism still lingered in Portugal (Doubleday).

The Golden Collar, Come Be My Guest, Shadows on the Water, and *The Fox from His Lair* are light, easy-reading novels with Portugal as the background, by Elizabeth Cadell. All but the first book (published by Thorndyke) are published by Morrow.

PORTUGAL'S PRESENT AND PAST

After Portugal's African colonies gained their independence, thousands of citizens returned, principally from Angola. This influx put a great strain on an already unstable economy. The years 1984 and 1985 saw a return of emigrants, mainly from France and Germany, who were encouraged to leave by those governments because of their own internal fiscal problems. For years, the money remitted by emigrants and investments they made in housing constituted a large part of the national income. That is no longer the case. However, many believe that the returned emigrants will enrich the country not only with capital but with new ideas, ambition, and the know-how and determination to get things done.

The democracy is fragile, yet the great majority of the population want it to succeed. In 1986, Portugal, a country with the lowest per capita income in Europe, entered the European Common Market, a move calculated to consolidate democracy and assure significant financial aid. Foreign investment is needed to develop industry and agriculture but investors have been hesitant because of political shakiness.

The chief stumbling block to agricultural development has been the predominance of very small family plots of land. More than 70 percent of Portuguese farms are smaller than 10 acres and these are often divided into several sub-plots. There is a movement toward pooling small farms into more efficient units.

Another great drain on Portugal is the import of all fuel oil. The search continues for alternate sources of energy. Most Portuguese oppose nuclear energy. In the central and southern parts of the country are areas having almost 3000 hours of sunshine a year and thus solar energy is being seriously considered there. More hydroelectric plants are being planned.

The visitor who takes time to explore Portugal in depth becomes emotionally involved and optimistic for the country's future, developing an empathy for the people, warming to their friendliness, marveling at their stoicism and diligence.

Some important dates in Portuguese history:

7000 B.C. Atlantic coast inhabited by humans.

1000 B.C. Celts begin series of invasions; several fortified stone towns, *citânias* or *castros,* remain; Citânia de Briteiros is the most famous (200 words of Celtic origin are still part of the Portuguese language).

900–700 B.C. Greeks and Phoenicians establish trading posts along coasts (unique style of Nazaré fishing boats is derived from Phoenicians); evidence of fertility cults seen in stone bears of Bragança and Murça and in present-day custom of exchanging cakes baked in shape of phalli during Amarante's Festa of São Gonçalo, patron saint of marriage.

300–200 B.C. Carthaginians invade peninsula, winter in the Algarve; their control ends with Rome's victory over Carthage in 202 B.C.

139 B.C. Lusitani tribal chieftain Viriatus leads rebellion against Romans; resistance ends with his death.

139 B.C.–600s A.D. Peninsula dominated by Rome; symbols of reign seen in excavations in Conímbriga, Temple of Diana in Evora, aqueduct of Elvas.

200s. Christianity spreads throughout Portugal.

400s. Germanic tribes invade peninsula; Alans, a tribe of Iranian stock, occupy central Portugal.

500–900s. Visigoths displace Romans as rulers.

711–1249. Moors from Africa invade and establish kingdoms in Spain; reign in Portugal not long-lasting and penetration into north trivial; left contributions to agriculture and to art in the use of glazed, painted tiles (*azulejos*).

800–900. Last Visigothic monarch, Pelayo, leads Reconquest from Asturias; Portucale, land north of Mondego River, liberated.

1139. Afonso Henriques proclaimed first king of Portugal as Afonso I; conducts Reconquest with fervor.

1249. Moorish occupation in Portugal ends.

1385. João I is victor over Spain in Battle of Aljubarrota.

1386. Treaty of Windsor begins Anglo-Portuguese alliance, the most enduring in European history.

1415. Portugal captures Ceuta, Morocco; Prince Henry starts school of navigation at Sagres.

1419. First voyage of discovery under sponsorship of Prince Henry.

1488. Bartolomeu Dias rounds Cape of Good Hope.

1494. Treaty of Tordesillas divides New World between Spain and Portugal.

1498. Sailing around Africa, Vasco da Gama discovers sea route to India.

1500. Pedro Cabral reaches Brazil and claims it for Portugal.

1578. Portuguese supremacy ends with Battle of El-Ksar-El-Kebir in Morocco, King Sebastião slain in battle.

1580. Philip II of Spain invades and proclaims himself King Felipe I of Portugal.

1640. Duke of Bragança leads revolt against Spain; takes title of João IV.

1668. Spain acknowledges Portugal's independence.

1755. Disastrous earthquake levels Lisboa.

1793. Portugal joins with England in first move against Napoleon's revolutionary government.

1807. Junot leads French troops in invasion of Portugal; royal family goes to Brazil in exile.

1808. Wellington arrives with British troops.

1810. French fighting in Portugal ends with Wellington's victory in Battle of Buçaco.

1834. Pedro IV, emperor of Brazil, emerges victor in Portugal's civil war, known as the War of the Two Brothers; forces extremist brother Miguel I to abdicate in favor of his daughter, Maria.

1908. King Carlos I and heir Luis Felipe are assassinated.

1910. Manoel II abdicates; Republic of Portugal proclaimed.

1910–28. Portugal sends troops against Germany in World War I; economic and political situation in Portugal deteriorates.

1932–68. António de Oliveira Salazar, former professor of economics, minister of finance in 1926 and 1928, assumes leadership of government and acts as dictator; suppresses opposition; supports Franco; remains neutral during World War II, although grants to England use of facilities in Azores; drafts constitution for the new state.

1968–74. Dr. Marcello Caetano, former rector of University of Lisboa, succeeds Salazar; amid demands for independence in Portuguese overseas territories and trouble in the military, government overthrown in bloodless coup in 1974.

1974. General Spínola becomes president in May; succeeded by Costa Gomes in September.

1975. 90 percent of electorate vote in general election on April 25; Socialist Party victorious; Rear-Admiral Azevedo becomes prime minister of fifth provisional government.

1975–77. Ramalho Eanes heads government.

1977–85. Portugal makes plans to join European Common Market. Controversy over nationalization of industries.

1986. Portugal joins the Common Market.

MONARCHS OF PORTUGAL

Afonso I (Afonso Henriques) (1139–85). Son of Henri of Burgundy and Teresa; after Henri's death, Teresa ruled, as regent for her son, a small region between the Douro and Minho rivers—Portucale; Afonso later rebelled against his mother in Battle of São Mamede in 1128; expanded territory south in battles against Moors, taking Lisboa, Evora, Alcácer, and Beja; recognized as ruler of kingdom of Portugal by papal bull of 1179; credited with founding new country. Tomb in Monastery of the Holy Cross in Coimbra.

Sancho I (1185–1211). Son of Afonso I; created many municipalities in eastern and central Portugal; attracted northern settlers because of privileges incorporated into charters; continued Reconquest; aided at times by Crusaders; tomb in Monastery of the Holy Cross in Coimbra.

AFONSO II (1211–23). Son of Sancho I; known as "the Fat" because childhood illness left him incapable of military rigors; tried to reclaim territory granted by father and grandfather to nobles and church.

SANCHO II (1223–46). Son of Afonso II; reign one of political confusion because of growing power of church; ordered dethroned by papal bull; left no legitimate heirs.

AFONSO III (1246–79). Brother of Sancho II; united divided kingdom; completed Reconquest; shifted capital from Coimbra to Lisboa; established power of throne over church; introduced commoners to early parliament called the Cortes.

DINIS (1279–1325). Son of Afonso III; known as the "Poet King" because of writing ability and the "Farmer King" because of encouragement and promotion of agriculture; built first Portuguese fleet; founded first university at Coimbra; declared dialect spoken in Porto official language of country; married to Isabel of Aragón, who was later canonized and known as Queen Saint Isabel because of devotion and service to poor; not of Isabel's purity, Dinis sired several illegitimate children.

AFONSO IV (1325–57). Son of Dinis and Isabel; remembered for his part in most tragic romance in Portuguese history—that of Inês de Castro and Afonso's son, Dom Pedro; joined with Spanish to defeat Muslims in last attempt to invade peninsula.

PEDRO I (1357–67). Son of Afonso IV; wreaked savage revenge on murderers of Inês de Castro; continued grandfather's separation of church and state; codified laws.

FERNANDO I (1367–83). Son of Pedro I and Constanza of Aragón; last of Burgundy dynasty; continued development of agriculture and maritime enterprises; Fernando died leaving no heir; tomb is in outside gallery of Monastery of Mafra.

JOAO I (1383–1433). Illegitimate son of Pedro I; led rebellion against Castilian conspiracy; master of the Order of Avis, João defeated the pretenders in 1385 at Battle of Aljubarrota; began construction of Monastery of Batalha; married Philippa of Lancaster, daughter of John of Gaunt, who gave him six children, most famous being Prince Henry the Navigator.

DUARTE (1433–38). Eldest son of João and Philippa; encouraged brothers in abortive attempt to conquer Tangier; during the battle, youngest brother Fernando taken prisoner—Duarte was embittered at failure to rescue brother, who died a prisoner six years later; Duarte buried in Alcobaça.

AFONSO V (1438–81). Son of Duarte; inherited throne at age six; Duarte's brother, Dom Pedro, ruled as regent until challenged by eldest bastard son of João I, Afonso, count of Barcelos, duke of Bragança; Afonso V married his cousin Isabel, daughter of Dom Pedro; encouraged Prince Henry in maritime activities; after Isabel's death, marrried Juana "La Beltraneja," daughter of Enrique IV of Castilla; became embroiled in difficulties with Ferdinand and Isabella because he claimed Castilian throne through Juana.

JOAO II (1481–95). Son of Afonso and Isabel; ruled during father's last years; rescinded privileges granted to nobles by father; during attempts to break enormous power of the Bragança family had the duke beheaded; continued the nation's maritime enterprises; kept trade control in royal hands; agreed to Treaty of Tordesillas, which divided New World between Spain and Portugal; left no heir.

MANOEL I (1495–1521). Cousin of João; married Isabel, eldest daughter of Ferdinand and Isabella; used unbelievable wealth pouring in from overseas colonies to develop new form of architecture called Manueline (see Glossary).

JOAO III (1521–57). Son of Manoel; pious and reticent, unable to resist Castilian influence of wife Catherine, sister of Castilla's Carlos V; allowed Catherine to run government; Inquisition installed in 1536.

SEBASTIAO I (1557–78). Grandson of João III; religious fanaticism resulted in disastrous battle against the infidels in Morocco; Battle of El-Ksar-El-Kebir ended Portugal's supremacy; Sebastião and scores of Portuguese aristocrats slain; rumors of his survival mushroomed into a cult known as Sebastianism.

HENRIQUE I (1578–80). Last surviving son of Manoel I and only heir to throne; his advanced age and former years as cardinal foretold end of the Avis dynasty. Laying claim to throne because mother had been sister of João III, Philip II of Spain, at death of Henrique, seized crown of Portugal: Spain ruled Portugal until 1641.

JOAO IV (1641–56). Duke of Bragança; led revolt against

Spanish domination; took title of João IV; encouraged by wife, Luisa, whose two sons were to become kings of Portugal and whose daughter Catherine would be Charles II's queen of England; João's reign known as the Restoration.

AFONSO VI (1656–83). Son of João; mother, Luisa, ruled as regent for the ten-year-old king; partially paralyzed from disease in infancy; believed to have been mentally impaired; persuaded to turn over government to brother, Pedro, who ruled as prince-regent from 1668 to 1683; Afonso spent last nine years of his life in Royal Palace at Sintra.

PEDRO II (1683–1706). Brother of Afonso VI; reign saw lessening of problems with Spain and signing of Methuen Treaty—an English, Dutch, Portuguese alliance.

JOAO V (1706–50). Son of Pedro II; well-educated, interested in mathematics and music; appointed ministers who ruled country effectively; used wealth from Brazilian gold mines to promulgate another architectural style called Joanine (see Glossary); reign termed Age of Absolutism because the Cortes was never convened and provinces were ruled by royal military command.

JOSE I (1750–77). Son of João V; fun-loving, shallow nature, little interest in political affairs; delegated power of government to Marques de Pombal, who, using despotic methods, accomplished reforms in education, spurred industry, encouraged the arts; Pombal responsible for rebuilding Lisboa after earthquake of 1775, expelling Jesuits from country and colonies, and weakening control of aristocracy.

MARIA I (1777–1816). Daughter of José I; married to José's brother, Dom Pedro (III); first years of reign peaceful; then emotional instability aggravated by deaths of husband, son, and other family members rendered her incapable of ruling; government turned over to second son, João, in 1792.

JOAO VI (1816–26). Ruled as prince-regent until mother's death; took royal family to Brazil when Napoleon's troops neared Lisboa; continued to rule from Brazil and advise council of regency while country struggled through Peninsular War; became estranged from wife, Carlota-Joaquina, who was obsessed with desire to rule and ambitious for younger son, Miguel; finally acceded to pressure to return to Portugal as country was bordering on revolution; son Pedro remained to rule Brazil as Pedro I.

PEDRO IV vs. MIGUEL I (1826–34). João's death triggered civil war known as the War of the Two Brothers; in Pedro's absence, absolutists contrived to have Miguel crowned king of Portugal. Urged to return by constitutionists, Pedro abdicated in favor of son, Pedro, who governed Brazil as Pedro II. Accompanied by daughter, Maria da Gloria, Pedro arrived to conduct the victorious struggle against Miguel, the usurper.

MARIA-DA-GLORIA (1834–53). Succeeded father, Pedro, at age 15; married to Ferdinand of Saxe-Coburg, cousin of Victoria's Prince Albert; disputes between moderates and radicals caused many changes of government; real problems—financial and economic—not resolved; died while giving birth to eleventh child.

PEDRO V (1853–61). Well educated and trained by parents Ferdinand and Maria; had strong sense of duty; showed promise of being competent ruler; died of typhoid fever, as did two younger brothers, in 1861.

LUIS I (1861–89). Brother of Pedro V; ascended throne at 23; was true constitutional monarch who left task of initiating legislation to political leaders; frequent changes of governments, civil strife led to growing disenchantment and republicanism gained ground.

CARLOS I (1889–1908). Son of Luis I; married to Amelie, daughter of Count of Paris; talented painter and extraordinary draftsman whose works may be seen in Palace of the Dukes of Bragança in Vila Viçosa; government on brink of bankruptcy; trouble fomented by groups of anarchists; Carlos and heir Luis Felipe assassinated in the Terriero do Paço in Lisboa.

MANOEL II (1908–10). Greatly shaken by murders of father and brother; not trained to rule; monarchist parties collapsed, leading to revolution of October 5, 1910; republic declared in Lisboa; Manoel and royal family debarked on yacht *Dona Amelia* for Gibraltar and England.

Places to Stay, Eat, and Visit

LISBOA

Historians trace the founding of this charming city built on seven hills overlooking the Tejo River to the Phoenicians. Romanticists believe the credit should go to Ulysses and cite as evidence the name Ulyssipona appearing on ancient maps.

Thirteenth-century B.C. Phoenicians called the port Alis Ubbo and developed it into an important trading center for ships en route to northern Europe. Then in succession came the Greeks, the Carthaginians, and the Romans.

When the glory of Rome faded, Visigoths arrived and prevailed until they were displaced by the Moors, during whose 300-year stay Lissibona strengthened its status as a thriving maritime city.

Crusaders on their way to the Holy Land helped Portugal's first king, Afonso Henriques, drive out the Moors in 1127. The city prospered to such an extent that in 1255 Afonso III decreed Lisboa rather than Coimbra capital of the country.

During the fifteenth and sixteenth centuries, Lisboa became one of the greatest commercial ports in the world, as huge quantities of riches from Asia, Africa, and Brazil poured into the harbor.

Affluence continued despite 60 years of Spanish rule in the first half of the seventeenth century. In 1640 João of Bragança ousted the Spanish and established the house of Avis, which ruled Portugal until 1910.

In the early years of the eighteenth century, João V ordered construction of the Aguas Livres Aqueduct. Twenty years were consumed in its erection and in 1748, the eleven-mile aqueduct, with 109 arches, began delivering water to Lisboa and continues to do so to this day.

On a sunny November morning in 1755, a devastating earthquake struck the city. It is estimated that as many as 40,000 lost their lives. Although damaged, the aqueduct survived, as did Lisboa's oldest structure, the Castelo de São Jorge, and the old Moorish section called the Alfama.

When the ineffective, distraught King José I asked his prime minister what should be done, the marquis of Pombal is said to have replied, "Bury the dead and feed the living."

Pombal was given carte blanche to rebuild the city. To this sometimes cruel, despotic planner belong accolades for the broad mosaic avenues, the *azulejo*-bedecked buildings, and the spacious *praças* highlighted by dramatic statuary that delight visitors.

There are so many things to see and do in Lisboa that it comes down to two considerations: time allotment and physical stamina. Day one could begin with a cab ride to the Museu Nacional dos Coches (coach museum). Housed in the former Riding Academy of Belém Palace is a wondrous collection of vehicles that transported royalty for three centuries. Among the historic carriages is a decorated black coach in which Philip II of Spain entered Lisboa in the winter of 1580 to rule Portugal.

Exit to the right and walk toward an enormous white edifice, Mosteiro dos Jerónimos (Jerónimo monastery, also called the Hieronymite monastery). Designed by the illustrious architect Boytac, it was ordered by Manoel I to commemorate the voyages of discovery soon after Vasco da Gama returned from the Indies in 1502. The building is lavishly Manueline in style, and successive architects have added decorations in their own styles. Tombs of the famous include those of Manoel I and João III and their queens, Vasco da Gama, and Camões. The Archeological Museum, in part of the west wing, contains Iberian and Roman artifacts.

Continue through the west wing to the Maritime Museum, where one becomes aware, perhaps for the first time, of the importance of Prince Henry the Navigator. It was this brilliant aesthete, driven by religious fervor to Christianize the world, who established a school of navigation to which he lured the finest intellects of the time. On an isolated peninsula at Sagres on the Algarve, his scholars developed the astrolabe and charted the seas. Columbus benefited from accomplishments of the school when he married the daughter of one of Henry's sea captains and inherited his father-in-law's maps and charts. The museum has an extensive collection of ship models from all periods, memorabilia from Portugal's African and Asian campaigns, and a cabin of the royal yacht *Dona Amelia*, which carrried the last royal family to Gibraltar and exile in 1910. Sumptuous furniture and elegant silver and china used by the monarchs are on display.

Connected to the Maritime Museum is a large hangar-type building whose severity is eased by lustrous stained glass windows. This is the room of the galleons that conveyed royalty down the Tejo River. One 1778 classic is replete with male mannequins in oaring readiness. It was retired in 1957 after the state visit of Elizabeth II and Philip of England.

Walk through gardens extending from the monastery and cross under a railroad bridge to reach the Monument to the Discoveries. This stunning sculptural work was erected along the Tejo in 1960 to honor the 500th anniversary of the death of Prince Henry, who commands the sculpted prow of a boat, gazing seaward. Among those following him are King Manoel I holding an armillary sphere, Camões clutching verses of his *Lusiads*, and Nuno Gonçalves, whose polyptych *Adoration of Saint Vincent* may be seen in the Museum of Ancient Art. Mosaic pavement encircling the base of the monument reveals a compass rose and a map of the world as known to Europeans in the fifteenth century.

From the monument is a view of graceful Salazar Bridge, longest in Europe and almost equal to San Francisco's Golden Gate. Look across the river at towering *Christ in Majesty*, a 92-foot replica of Rio de Janeiro's much larger statue.

Now stroll along the waterfront in the direction of the Tower of Belém. Delicious aromas emanating from small cafes will convince you it's time for an unforgettable *almoço* of crisp fried fish, salad laced with piquant dressing, and crunchy Portuguese bread, accompanied by a bottle of any kind of wine the *senhor* suggests. This repast will fortify you for the climb to the top of the five-story Tower of Belém.

Although it now stands at water's edge, imagine the tower in the middle of the river, as it stood defending Lisboa in 1520. It saw departures and returns of such explorers as Vasco da Gama. The handsome structure has a pleasing amount of Manueline embellishment. On one terrace is a particularly lovely statue of the Virgin, *Our Lady of Safe Homecoming*.

That's enough for one day.

Day two could begin by walking along Avenida da Liberdade to Praça Marques de Pombal. A statue of the rebuilder of Lisboa dominates the *praça*. It takes several short street crossings to reach the spectacular stairway of gardens leading to Edward VII Park, named in honor of the English king's visit to the city in 1902. Within the park are a children's playground, a lake, the Estufa Fria greenhouse of exotic tropical vegetation, and a stage where ballet and classical music concerts are performed outdoors during the summer. This makes a nice half-day excursion.

On another day walk south along Avenida da Liberdade. An obelisk in the center of the Praça dos Restauradores pays homage to those "restorers" who achieved freedom from Spain in 1640. Praça Dom Pedro IV is called the Rossio by natives. The square was in existence in the thirteenth century and was the scene of many autos-da-fé during the Inquisition. Pombal is responsible for its present aspect. Among the eighteenth- and nineteenth-century structures is Dona Maria II National Theater. Built in 1840 on the site of the former Palace of the Inquisition, it is topped with a statue of Gil Vicente, who originated Portuguese drama. Also on the *praça* is the Rossio train station. In the center, between two fountains, is an altered bronze statue of King Pedro IV, later crowned king of Brazil as Pedro I. The story goes that in reality it was a statue of Maximilian in the process of being delivered to Mexico. When news of his assassination arrived, authorities on both sides quickly made a deal. Lisboa got a statue at a very good price. Many shops and outdoor cafes rim the *praça*.

Now the route divides into short streets east and west of Praça dos Restauradores. Rua Aurea, Rua Augusta, and Rua Prata house many of the outstanding shops in this main commercial area of Lisboa.

Ultimately, by heading south, you will arrive in one of the most beautiful and spacious squares in the world, Praça do Comercio, also called Terreiro do Paço (palace terrace) and Black Horse Square. Machado de Castro's equestrian statue of King José I has the place of honor, facing the Tejo River. The square's other three sides are lined with handsome arcaded buildings dating from Pombal's time. An arch of triumph completes the grandeur.

Another day's tour should include Castelo São Jorge (Saint George's castle), the Sé (cathedral), and the Alfama. You can either start at the top of the citadel with the castle, or at the bottom with the Sé and Alfama.

The castle is called the Cradle of Lisboa because its lofty locale held fortresses of the Romans, Visigoths, and Moors. Ten towers, joined by massive walls, were reinforced by Afonso I after his victory over the Moors. Manoel I made further reconstructions of the castle, which served as royal headquarters from the fourteenth to the sixteenth centuries. Now there are lovely gardens and gentle fountains. The belvederes offer wonderful views of the city. A tiled picture-map is especially helpful in identifying landmarks. It is easy to locate the ruins of the Carmo Convent and the unique outdoor Santa Justa elevator built by Gustave Eiffel.

RESTAURANTE CASA DO LEÃO. Have lunch in the Restaurante Casa do Leão. Once an eighteenth-century *adega* (wine cellar) of the castle, it now houses a luxurious eatery. During conversion of the *adega,* a brick ceiling from the fourteenth or fifteenth century was uncovered and it now lends warm tones to the decor. Colorful *azulejos* were added during construction. On cool days apéritifs are served in front of a cozy fireplace.

The menu is continental and Portuguese. Smoked swordfish makes an excellent hors d'oeuvres. Choose from various entrees such as sole, sea bass, shrimp, *bacalhau,* roast duck, or chateaubriand with bearnaise sauce. The wine list is extensive and includes all of Portugal's finest. This unique restaurant is owned by the state and managed by ENATUR. The phone number is 87-59-62.

After lunch, walk down from the castle to the Museum of Decorative Arts, set up in 1953 to preserve the traditional skills of crafters. You will be given a guided tour of 21 workshops where restorative activities are in progress.

You will enjoy rambling through the Alfama, the oldest district in Lisboa, a cobbled maze of white-washed dwellings adorned with wrought iron balconies and splendid *azulejos.* Tiny vegetable and fish shops, bars and cafes, small *praças* edged with sixteenth-century houses, remnants of old city walls and gates, and appealing churches will hold your attention for hours.

The Sé, or cathedral, is below the Castelo to the west of the Alfama. It was built on the site of an Arab mosque shortly after Afonso's rout of the Moors. Two crenellated towers indicate that the cathedral has also been a fortress. Although rebuilt after several earthquakes down through the centuries, the cathedral retains a Romanesque appearance.

You can either board one of the quaint trolleys passing the cathedral to return to the Praça do Comercio or take a taxi.

Portugal was the fortunate recipient of the fabulous wealth of Calouste Gulbenkian, a Turkish-born Armenian who, although a British citizen, chose to spend the last 13 years of his life in Portugal. The Gulbenkian Museum is one of the finest in the world, beautifully displaying the wide variety of art this one man spent a lifetime acquiring. Not only the art collection but practically all of his quite considerable estate, derived mostly from his 5 percent interest in the Iraq Petroleum Company, comprises the Gulbenkian Foundation, whose purpose is to endow and encourage scientific, educational, artistic, and charitable works. The museum is only one part of the complex. There are three auditoriums, a library, an open-air theater, and lecture rooms. Spend a whole morning enjoying fantastic riches, then walk to the nearby Lisboa Sheraton for lunch in the rooftop Panorama Restaurant. The menu is extensive and diverse, even offering U.S.-style hamburgers. Savor delicious food while pinpointing from on high the neighborhoods and monuments you have visited.

The Museum of Ancient Art is located on Rua das Janelas Verdes (street of the green windows). The principal masterpiece to see here is the famous polyptych of Nuno Gonçalves. Painted between 1460 and 1470, the six panels of the *Adoration of Saint Vincent* portray many figures in Portuguese history, from Saint Vincent to Queen Saint Isabel to Prince Henry the Navigator.

YORK HOUSE HOTEL. Also on Rua Janelas Verdes is York House Hotel, a complex consisting of a former sixteenth-century convent and just down the street, a three-story house built in the 1500s. The latter is referred to as York House Residencia. For those who prefer the intimacy of a small hotel when in a large city, York House may be the answer. The 18 guest rooms in the house are charmingly furnished in Portuguese Victorian style. Only breakfast is served in the Residencia. Other meals are taken down the street at the 50-room former convent. Rooms there are more simply, but still adequately, furnished. There is no menu at meal time. Guests are served soup, salad, entree, and dessert. It is plain food, but tasty and nourishing. Prices at York House are extremely reasonable. (Rua Janelas Verdes 47, phone 66-81-44.)

Getting to know Lisboa becomes exciting. If possible, spend a few days at the beginning and the end of your Portuguese or Iberian trip for a lasting appreciation of an exceptional city.

Hotel Albatroz

CASCAIS

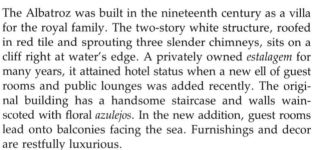

***** govt. rating
37 rooms, swimming pool, underground garage
Phone 28-28-21

DIRECTIONS: 31 km west of Lisboa.

The Albatroz was built in the nineteenth century as a villa
for the royal family. The two-story white structure, roofed
in red tile and sprouting three slender chimneys, sits on a
cliff right at water's edge. A privately owned *estalagem* for
many years, it attained hotel status when a new ell of guest
rooms and public lounges was added recently. The original building has a handsome staircase and walls wainscoted with floral *azulejos*. In the new addition, guest rooms
lead onto balconies facing the sea. Furnishings and decor
are restfully luxurious.

In the bar, open at 11 A.M., snacks and sandwiches may
be ordered. Hours in the seaside indoor and outdoor dining rooms are 12:30–3 P.M. and 7:30–10 P.M. The menu is
continental and Portuguese and all items are a la carte.
Interesting dishes include poached salmon, roast kid, chateaubriand, partridge stew with applesauce, and duck with
orange sauce. Among dessert choices are crepes suzette.

For a double room facing the sea, prices range from 5900
escudos to 13,200 escudos.

The coast route north from Lisboa goes through Estoril,
one-time haven for exiled European royalty. It is now a

popular resort; the casino can be seen from the road. Six kilometers farther north is Cascais, bustling with activity. Gaily painted fishing boats share harbor and beach with vacationers.

To enjoy an outing to Cascais by train from Lisboa, take a taxi to the Cais do Sodré station in Lisboa. For less than 100 escudos you will arrive in Cascais in about 30 minutes. Don't worry about when to get off, as Cascais is the end of the line. As you depart the train station, you are within easy walking distance of the Albatroz (look for the red roof) and of the Atlantis crystal outlet. For the crystal shop, head down a side street branching off from the train *praça* in a one o'clock direction if emerging from the train station.

Hotel Palácio dos Seteais

2710 SINTRA

***** govt. rating
18 rooms, gardens
Phone 923-32-00

DIRECTIONS: 30 km northwest of Lisboa. After entering Sintra, motorists should follow signs reading Seteais and in a few minutes drive through gates to the hotel, set at the far end of an expanse of lawn.

Built in the late eighteenth century by the Dutch consul to Lisboa, the two rectangular buildings of gray stone are joined by an arch constructed in 1802 to commemorate the visit of the prince and princess of Brazil, later to become King João VI and Queen Carlota-Joaquina. The hotel occupies the wing to the left of the archway.

Some of the furniture is original. Glistening chandeliers hang from 15-foot ceilings. Intricate designs have been painted on plaster walls. A garden bordered by clipped hedges leads to a belvedere that has a view over a valley of small farms and villages.

The dining room is known for its excellent cuisine, drawing busloads of travelers who enjoy fine food in picturesque historic surroundings.

The building is traditionally regarded as the scene of the

armistice ceremony after Wellington's victory over the French in 1808. The terms were so favorable to the French that the Portuguese sarcastically dubbed the structure the "House of the Seven Sighs" (*sete ais*). Generations of aristocrats lived in the mansion until its conversion into a hotel. Although owned by the state, the *palácio* is managed by a private consortium.

SINTRA AND ENVIRONS. Sintra gained world-wide fame through the lyric praises of nineteenth-century poets. Gil Vicente, the great Portuguese dramatist, called Sintra

> A garden of the earthly paradise
> Sent here by Solomon
> To a Portuguese king.

Hills of pine, oak, and fern, periodically shrouded in dense fog from the Atlantic, keep Sintra cool and inviting even in the heat of summer. It had long been a retreat for royalty and today is a summer haven for affluent citizens of Lisboa.

To the south, Pena Palace soars from the highest point in the Serra de Sintra and is seen from the hotel entrance. Its present form dates from 1840, when it was constructed by Fernando II around ruins of a sixteenth-century monastery. The bizarre amalgamation of Arab gate, Manueline entry replete with scaly crocodile gargoyles, and Gothic arches contains a chapel and cloisters of the monastery. Rooms house carved furniture from India, tables, desks, and chairs inlaid with mother-of-pearl from Macao, Dresden chandeliers, Chinese porcelain vases, and large free-standing candelabra. Ceilings are embellished profusely with ethereal paintings. The guided tour includes bedrooms and baths of former queens and their attendants. Don't miss the commode beautified with gold medallions. An exquisite light fixture completes the feminine touch. A sun dial on the queen's balcony ignited the fuse of a small cannon at 5 P.M. daily. From the parking lot looking seaward notice a distant statue of the palace architect, German Count Eschwege, who, wearing a suit of mail, seems to be guarding the mountaintop.

The village of Sintra clusters around the Royal Palace (Palácio Real), also called the National Palace. It is distinguished by two tall conical chimneys. João I began construction on the site of an Arab palace at the end of the fourteenth century. He is responsible for the pointed arches, Moorish windows, and unique chimneys of the central portion. In the sixteenth century, Manoel I added the right wing and square tower to the north. For many centuries the palace served as a summer residence for Portuguese royalty.

The rooms are tiled with florid *azulejos*. Furniture inlaid with ivory is from Goa. Large soup tureens in a variety of shapes, including hippopotamuses, rest on long tables and credenzas along the walls. A fountain in the Arab Room is encircled with pillows as if for the comfort of moguls.

Sala dos Brasões (room of the coats of arms) has a multicolored domed ceiling, a combination of Christian and Moorish elements painted with the crests of Portugal's noble families.

In the Sala da Audiência, Camões read his *Lusiads* to young King Sebastião. It was in the Sala dos Cisnes, whose coffered ceiling holds octagonal panels decorated with paintings of swans, that the council of state approved the expedition that ended so disastrously at El-Ksar-El-Kebir, Morocco.

An amusing tale explains the genesis of the Magpie Room. João I married Philippa of Lancaster, daughter of John of Gaunt. Philippa was a proper gentlewoman who took a dim view of João's wandering eye. When she caught him planting a kiss upon the lips of one of her ladies-in-waiting, she raised an uproar. In retaliation, irate João ordered the ceiling painted with as many magpies as there were gossiping court ladies—136. Each magpie is uttering "por bem," whose literal translation is "for good." This doesn't make much sense in English in the twentieth century but undoubtedly raised some eyebrows in the fourteenth.

The kitchen holds the answer to the tremendous chimneys. It is about 100 feet long, 40 feet wide, and 90 feet high. Along one side of the white-tiled room are stoves bearing giant black iron kettles. A wall at one end contains ovens with several baking racks each. Beneath the chimneys are spits large enough to have roasted whole steers.

Sintra's market day is held on the second and fourth Sundays of each month. The great Saint Peter's Fair is held annually on June 29.

Restaurante Cozinha Velha

PALACIO NACIONAL DE QUELUZ
QUELUZ

***** govt. rating
Restaurant only; no lodgings
Phones 88-90-70, 88-90-78, 88-90-79

DIRECTIONS: 12 km southeast of Sintra.

The one-time kitchen of this palace, located in the north wing, which faces a statue of Maria I, is now an elegant Portuguese restaurant. A long stone work table holds pastry and hors d'oeuvres masterpieces. Huge copper kettles stand ready in the fireplace, which has a vaulted timber ceiling. Whole steers and deer could have been roasted on long spits. Stunning floral arrangements and recessed shelves exhibiting antique copper culinary accessories are nice touches.

The food is marvelous and the wine list comprehensive. Wear the best clothes you have along, as the dining room is rather formal in the afternoon, and more so at night. Highly recommended is the smoked swordfish appetizer garnished with finely chopped onion, grated hardboiled egg, and capers. The liver entree is superb as is a pine-apple-coconut whipped cream cake. *Planalto*, a white wine from SOGRAPE (a firm that exports Mateus rosé), is highly satisfying. (Open daily 1–3 P.M. and 7:30–10 P.M.)

TOURING QUELUZ. A community once built by the Moors and later destroyed by Afonso Henriques in 1147, Queluz's claim to fame is that it was an estate for royalty. The palace was built for Infante Dom Pedro, later husband of Maria I and younger son of João V, in the eighteenth century. One of many royal residences, this was inspired by Versailles. Extensive gardens on two levels were designed in 1762 in the style of the seventeenth-century French landscape architect Le Nôtre. A canal banked with yellow and purple *azulejos* is spanned by a bridge reminiscent of Venice. Statues of Neptune command reflective pools.

Visitors are taken on guided tours through the palace, where floors are of inlaid Brazilian woods and walls are covered with silk. In each room are priceless objets d'art. Gold-trimmed gowns, shoes, and jewelry of queens and princesses are on display. The palace of Queluz (the name means "what light") is used today for official government receptions. The palace has been the scene of many events, among them the residence in exile of Carlota-Joaquina, wife of João VI, after being banished from court; the conspiracy of Pedro II to have his brother Afonso VI declared unfit to rule; and the death of Francisco, son of Pedro II, by choking on an oyster—his ghost is said to wander the palace grounds in expiation for the sin of gluttony.

MAFRA

The basilica and fluted domes of Mafra's enormous monastery (35 km north of Sintra) may be seen for miles. In 1708 João V vowed to erect a monastery if heaven would grant him a child. Feeling fairly confident, he purchased ten acres in Mafra, and began construction when his daughter was born in 1717.

Thirteen years were consumed in building the palace, monastery, and basilica, which have a total of 4500 windows and doors. German, Italian, and Portuguese architects utilized Carrara marble from Italy, woods from Brazil, and bells from Belgium. João hired so many artists that he decided to found a school of sculpture. Masterpieces of the students flood the buildings. One of the most illustrious graduates was Machado de Castro, whose works are seen in Lisboa as well as at Mafra.

Imposing larger-than-life statues of saints are placed on

The library of the monastery in Mafra.

recessed pedestals in an arcaded loggia. Different shades of marble form patterns on exterior and interior floors of the rambling edifice. Pink and smoky blue marble lend warmth to the basilica.

The palace contains some of the original furniture, including cradles of long-dead princes and princesses. The monastery housed as many as 300 monks at one time. Several of their cells are open for view. Most impressive is the Baroque library of more than 35,000 gold-illuminated volumes from the fourteenth and fifteenth centuries. The tomb of Fernando I, who died in 1383, rests in an open courtyard outside the basilica.

Historians contend that João's architectural excess at Mafra, whose cost is impossible to ascertain and into which rained wealth from Brazilian diamond mines, was a major factor in the beginning of Portugal's decline, even though it predated Lisboa's ruinous earthquake.

Today, parts of the monastery serve as army barracks, while the royal hunting preserve so favored by King Carlos is used as a military riding school.

Pousada do Castelo
OBIDOS, 2510 LEIRIA

CH govt. rating
9 rooms, gardens
Phone (Caldas da Rainha) 95105
Telex 15540

Estalagem do Convento
OBIDOS

** govt. rating
13 rooms, restaurant
Phone (Caldas da Rainha) 95217

DIRECTIONS TO THE POUSADA: 134 km north of Lisboa. Drive up Obidos's narrow main street almost to the crest. When you see a sign with a P on it, *don't* turn through the arch (the P stands for *paragem*, bus stop); go straight ahead and park on either side of the street. You must walk up to the pousada to register, and then a young attendant will help carry luggage.

Tucked in a corner of a medieval fortress dominating a walled village, this fifteenth-century palace, destroyed in the 1755 earthquake, was rebuilt as a pousada in 1951. Eighteenth-century antiques, including high leather-backed chairs and ornately carved furniture, grace guest rooms, hallways, and the reception lobby. The dining room is wainscoted with tiles, hand-painted in sepia on beige in various designs. A plate rail holds typical blue Portuguese ceramics, copper, brass, and pewter ware. A Manueline border rims the oversized fireplace. Should a sudden power outage occur, waiters are adept in providing instant candlelight, lending a romantic aura to dining.

The pousada is known for its good food. Entrees include *bacalhau à pousada* (baked cod), *frango na púcara* (chicken en casserole), *escalopes de vitela com cogumelos* (veal steak with mushrooms), and *ananás com presunto* (ham with pineapple). Dessert specialties are *tarte de amêndoa* (almond tart), *tarte de maçã* (apple tart), and *pudim de limão* (lemon pudding). Wines to consider are a sparkling Bairrada and red or white Alcobaça or Torres Vedras.

Because of the pousada's limited number of rooms, a prior reservation is essential. Should you arrive a day early or five minutes too late, consider Estalagem do Convento, down the hill. It is a comfortable inn with small but adequate rooms with baths, a bar, and a good restaurant.

TOURING OBIDOS. Obidos is a charming town of small whitewashed houses whose windows and balconies explode with cascading, riotous bougainvillea, geraniums, and impatiens. Santa Maria Church on the main square saw the marriage of ten-year-old King Afonso V and his eight-year-old cousin, Isabella, in 1444. Next to the church is a museum established by the Gulbenkian Foundation. The museum houses architectural and archeological relics, a collection of paintings, and a room devoted to Peninsular War memorabilia.

The Romans and Moors knew the strategic value of Obidos for guarding against attack from the sea. Today, however, after centuries of silting, Obidos lies 5 km from the water.

Afonso Henriques took the fortress from the Moors in 1148. Obidos means always faithful; the town got its name when it backed Sancho II against his ambitious brother, who was later to become Afonso III.

In 1228, King Dinis and young Queen Isabel visited the town, and she thought it so delightful that Dinis began reconstruction of castle remains and then "gave" the town to Isabel. This royal gesture became traditional with Portuguese rulers until 1833.

In 1491 the Infante, son of João II and Queen Leonor, had a fatal accident. His body was lost in the Tejo River until recovered in a fisherman's net. The distraught queen traveled to "her" town of Obidos in sorrow. The town pillory was built with a net on top to commemorate the tragedy. You must use your imagination as time has practically obliterated the net.

During the Peninsular War, Wellington reached Obidos, from whose ramparts he observed the French army in Rolica, eight miles away. The armies met, with the British-Portuguese troops winning the first but inconclusive conflict. Four days later, after receiving reinforcements, Wellington was victor in Vimeiro, 20 miles north of Obidos.

PENICHE

Peniche is one of Portugal's busiest fishing ports. Catches of tunny, crayfish, and sardines are canned in factories of the town. Boat building is also an important industry of Peniche.

Its location on a rocky promontory 24 km west of Obidos is distinguished by a sixteenth-century citadel that once boasted 100 heavy guns at the ready. During the Salazar regime, political dissidents were imprisoned in the fort and it later served as a temporary refuge for destitute Angolans.

The lace of Peniche, fashioned by women of the town since the eighteenth century, is justly famous and is for sale in several shops.

The Festival of Nossa Senhora da Boa Viagem (Our Lady of the safe journey) is held for three days in the first week of August. Festivities begin on Saturday evening with the solemn procession to the sea. On the next day, thousands of devout gather to witness the procession of Senhora da Boa Viagem, which includes, in addition to the statue of the Virgin, many colorful allegorical figures. After the religious phase of the fair, there are a folk dance festival, sports events, variety shows, and exhibitions of local handcrafts, featuring, naturally, bone lace.

NAZARÉ

In the fourth century, a monk brought a statue of the Virgin from the town of Nazareth to a small community of fishing familiies said to be descendants of the Phoenicians. Thus the name Nazaré was bestowed on what would become one of the most widely photographed fishing villages in the world, 37 km north of Obidos.

One of the reasons for its popularity with camera buffs is that there is no natural harbor. Boats must be rolled over logs into the breaking waves. In the past, oxen were used to beach returning boats, but today tractors perform the task. Otherwise, working life along the beaches of Nazaré has changed little over the centuries despite crowds of staring tourists.

Color is the outstanding element of Nazaré, beginning with an emerald sea frothing onto a rich beige shore strewn with vivid-hued boats, whose bows are decorated with large glaring "eyes." Older men retain traditional dress: black "Phoenician" cap whose tail trails over their shoulders almost to the waist, black pleated shirt, black trousers, and sandals. Some older women also wear black. Young women wear brilliant scarves tied on their heads in unique fashion, billowing skirts that reach just below the knee, and reputedly seven petticoats. At least three are visible as they scurry barefoot along the shore.

On days when the seas are too rough for small boats, larger vessels may venture forth, sometimes forced to return to Nazaré's alternate port, São Martinho do Porto, about 18 km south. Occasionally the local coast guard is called upon to guide boats to safety through crashing breakers. Their seamanship is a sight to see.

From the eighth to the fifteenth of September, local inhabitants and visitors participate in the Festival of Nossa Senhora da Nazaré, which features religious ceremonies, bullfights, folk dance groups, and handcraft exhibitions.

Caldas da Raínha, a noted ceramics center, is on the road between Obidos and Nazaré. The distinctive green and yellow pottery comes in many shapes, such as snails, lobsters, crabs, and caricature figures. Caldas da Raínha means hot springs of the queen. The town got its name from an incident in the fifteenth century. King João and Queen Leonor were traveling to Batalha in observance of the anniversary of the death of João's father, Afonso V, when the queen noticed people bathing in malodorous waters near the road. When she learned that the waters were helpful to those suffering from rheumatism, as she was, she immediately joined the bathers and legend says that she departed completely cured. There is a handsome statue of the rainha on the route through town.

Incidentally, when your nose suspects a town might have sewer problems, you will discover that there are termas or balnearios, health spas, in the vicinity. Portugal has some of the finest mineral springs in the world.

The monastery of Alcobaça.

ALCOBAÇA

The Alcoa and Baça rivers meet in a pleasant agricultural region of fruit trees and vineyards, and have given their names to a community 32 km northeast of Obidos which has been in existence since the eighth century.

After a victorious campaign against the Moors in 1147, Afonso I gave Alcobaça and the surrounding area to the Cistercian order of monks, thus fulfilling a vow he had made to Saint Bernard. Thirty years later, construction was begun on the site of a Moorish castle. The reputation of Santa Maria Monastery as one of the wealthiest and most influential religious centers in Portugal lasted for over 700 years.

Because of reconstructions during the seventeenth and eighteenth centuries, only the main entrance and rose window are original. The church is the largest in the country—the austerity of its high-vaulted interior is impressive.

Upstairs are the great monks' hall and the kitchen that turned out such vast amounts of food that an English visitor in the late eighteenth century termed the monastery "the most distinguished temple of gluttony in all Europe." Through the center of the kitchen, 60 feet in diameter, ran a stream of crystal water stocked with many kinds of river fish. Reconstructed in the eighteenth century, today the kitchen is lined with white and blue *azulejos*. The immense chimneys and massive marble work tables stand to remind visitors of meals that were prepared here for more than 500 monks and guests.

But the essential reason for journeying to Alcobaça is to pay homage before the tombs of Portugal's most famous lovers, Inês de Castro and Dom Pedro I, whose romantic legend Camões extolled in several episodes of the *Lusiads*.

Infanta Constanza of Aragón arrived in Lisboa in 1340 for her marriage to Dom Pedro, son of Afonso IV. She was accompanied by a lovely Galician lady in waiting, Inês de Castro, who immediately caught the attention of the new bridegroom. Afonso sought to prevent his son's amorous adventure by banishing Inês from court.

Dom Pedro traveled periodically to the Spanish town of Alburquerque, where Inês lived. When Constanza died in 1345 after giving birth to Fernando, Inês returned to Portugal. Dom Pedro installed her in a country house in Coimbra, Quinta das Lagrimas (house of tears). The romance progressed so successfully that several children were born to the blissful couple.

In the meantime, Afonso and his nobles were increasingly concerned that the brothers of Inês were plotting against Portugal. At length, Afonso was persuaded that Inês must go. He looked the other way when three men ambushed and stabbed her to death on January 7, 1355.

The enraged Pedro, aided by Inês's brothers, who had invaded from Galicia, tried to stage a rebellion against his father. The battles raged for many months until a defeated Pedro was forced to swear he would not wreak vengeance upon Inês's murderers.

However, his chance came within two years, when he

attained the throne after the death of his father. His first act was to seek the assassins. He was able to capture two of the three. Forsaking his vow, he ordered the most cruel executions possible. One's heart was drawn out through his chest, the other's through his back.

Then, stating that he and Inês had been secretly wed, he ordered her body exhumed, clothed in coronation robes, and crowned, and forced members of the court to parade by her bier, each planting a kiss on the decayed hand of his "queen."

The tombs of the lovers lie toward the front of the church, Pedro's to the right of the altar and Inês's to the left. They are placed so that on Resurrection Day, they will "rise" to face each other. On their tombs is inscribed "Ate ao fim do mundo"—until the end of the world. Carved in the fourteenth century, the tombs are splendidly ornate. Despite the fact that the tip of Inês's nose is missing thanks to boorish destruction by French troops in 1811, the sculpture still conveys her classic beauty.

Footnote to romance: The "inconsolable" Pedro was able to assuage his grief through an affair with Teresa Lourenço. Less than three years after the murder of Inês, Teresa gave birth to a son, João, who in time established the royal dynasty of the house of Avis.

Pousada do Mestre Afonso Domingues

2440 BATALHA

C govt. rating
19 rooms, 1 suite
Phone 96260, 96261
Telex 42339

DIRECTIONS: 20 km northeast of Alcobaça.

The attractive roadside inn had been a private estalagem until acquired by the state in 1985. Carpeted rooms are comfortably furnished with twin or double beds, desk-commode, and occasional chairs. Adjoining tiled baths are roomy and functional. Food in the pleasant dining room is excellent, one reason for the popularity of the pousada. A gracious gesture of placing the flag of each diner's coun-

try on the table further enhances enjoyment of superb cuisine.

Several shops and markets cluster round the pousada. Fine bedspreads, linens, and sweaters are hung outside to lure shoppers.

SANTA MARIA DA VITORIA MONASTERY. Another reason for the popularity of the pousada is its proximity to Santa Maria da Vitória Monastery, a masterpiece of Portuguese architecture. The pousada is named for one of the original architects of the monastery. Begun in 1402 and completed in 1428, its construction was in compliance to a vow made by João I on the eve of the Battle of Aljubarrota.

João, the bastard son of Pedro and Teresa Lourenço, made a name for himself when he broke into the palace in Lisboa and murdered a count who was scheming to have King Juan of Castilla take charge of the government. João took the title defender of the realm, and he and his followers determined to expel the pretender Juan. When news of João's bold act spread throughout the country, uprisings against Spanish sympathizers occurred in Porto, Evora, and other towns. Nuno Alvares Pereira, commander of the defender's troops, drove the Spanish from the Alentejo. It is Pereira's equestrian statue that one sees from the pousada.

João was proclaimed king in 1385. In August, Spanish and Portuguese armies met at Aljubarrota, 15 km south of Batalha. Despite overwhelming odds, Alvares was victor in the decisive battle, which resulted in 200 years of independence from Spain.

Vandalized by the French in 1810 and damaged by fire in 1811, the monastery was abandoned by the Dominicans following the abolition of religious orders in 1834. With water damage and ceilings in danger of collapse, stripped of its stained glass windows, the monument was saved by Fernando II and restorations continue to this day.

It was João who ordered construction of the church, founder's chapel, the first cloister, and the chapterhouse. Subsequent rulers added other portions, but the whole was never finished because when it was Manoel's turn he devoted all his time, attention, and wealth to Belém.

To the right upon entering the founder's chapel are the tombs of João and his wife Philippa of Lancaster, who lie hand-in-hand beneath an octagonal stone canopy on which are carved the coats of arms of Avis and Lancaster. The tombs of their illustrious children circle João's and Philippa's.

The royal cloister is an elegant example of Gothic and Manueline architecture. Portugal's tomb of the unknown soldiers (one from Africa, the other from Flanders) is in the chapterhouse. The memorial is reverently simple, with two wreaths, an eternal flame, and *Christ of the Trenches*, a statue presented to the country by France in 1958.

Estalagem Dom Gonçalo

2495 FATIMA

**** govt. rating
43 rooms, elevator, garage
Phone 97262, 97263
Telex 43838 GONTEL

DIRECTIONS: 13 km southeast of Batalha. If entering Fátima from Batalha, you will see the *estalagem* on the left just past a roundabout.

Built in 1982, this inn is on the outskirts of the hustle and bustle that is Fátima once every month, especially in May and October. In addition to well-appointed guest rooms, there is a bar-lounge, a large TV room with fireplace, a gift shop, and an inviting dining room. The wine list is quite extensive and the menu features three-course luncheons and dinners. Double-room prices include breakfast and are very reasonable at 3000 escudos. You can eat lunch or dinner, including coffee and wine, for under US$10.

Fátima is called the Lourdes of Portugal. Catholics from all over the world visit the shrine that evolved from these events: On May 13, 1917, three children were tending a flock of sheep at Cova da Iria near the village of Fátima. Suddenly the skies were illuminated and the Virgin appeared, speaking a message of peace. The vision was repeated six times until October 13. It was reported that 70,000 people witnessed this last apparition.

Pilgrimages of the faithful were made to the locale in ever-increasing numbers. On May 13, 1928, the archbishop of Evora laid the first stone of the future basilica. On October 13, 1930, the bishop of Leiria gave official recognition to the cult of Our Lady of Fátima.

Although visits continue throughout the year, large groups of Portuguese are seen along roads leading to and from Fátima on the twelfth and thirteenth of each month. They struggle forward, some barefoot, some with canes and crutches. Men carry large bundles on their backs. Women balance similar burdens on their heads. They will stay in town for a few days, either camping out or being taken in by residents. It is said that those giving shelter to pilgrims are rewarded with blessings.

It is an emotional experience to watch the devout of all ages make obeisance to the basilica and back, a distance of some 1000 feet on their knees over tesselated pavement. Inclement weather is no deterrent.

Pousada de São Pedro
CASTELO DO BODE, 2300 TOMAR

B govt. rating
16 rooms, gardens
Phone (Torres Novas) 38175
Telex 42392

DIRECTIONS: 66 km southeast of Batalha, 13 km southeast of Tomar. 7 km east of Highway N-110.

The pousada overlooks a gravity dam in a tranquil wooded area. Reception hall, public lounges, bar, dining room, and eight guest rooms are located in the main building. A few yards away is an annex with another eight rooms and baths.

The pousada offers a comfortable stay in secluded natural surroundings and is popular with water sports enthusiasts. The reservoir provides opportunities for fishing, rowing, sailing, motorboating, and waterskiing. From the road over the dam, look down on the Zêzere River winding through rocky terrain where hillsides are planted in olive groves.

A large picture window of the dining room affords a view of the reservoir and dam. Entrees include *pregado com molho de tomate* (turbot with tomato sauce), *pato no forno com laranja* (roast duck with orange sauce), *lombos de pescada com molho de tomate* (slices of whiting with tomato sauce), and *lombo de porco com laranja* (pork loin with orange). Besides well-known wines, a regional *tinto* from Tomar will appeal.

SIDE TRIPS FROM CASTELO DO BODE. The pousada is a good base from which to visit Tomar, humming with activity and site of the Convent of Christ. (Tomar is also accessible by train from Lisboa.) Signs through town point the way to the Convento. Before ascending the hill, pause at Praça do Infante Henrique for a look at the statue of austere Henry the Navigator, which stands before iron gateways to a beautiful park that is complete with a fish-filled stream, old water wheel, and sycamores alive with chattering birds.

Once at the convent, motorists should leave their car in a designated area and walk through an archway to the church grounds. Old convent buildings up the hill to the right now house a military hospital.

In 1160 the grand master of the Order of the Knights Templar began building a fortified castle whose original protective walls still encircle the summit of the convent grounds. When Pope Clement V in 1314 yielded to pressure from European monarchs complaining the order was becoming too powerful and disbanded the organization throughout the continent, King Dinis merely changed the name to Order of Knights of Christ. It became an influential national military-religious order. Prince Henry was grand master from 1418 to 1460 and channeled much of its wealth into financing the voyages of discovery.

The most unusual feature of the church is the twelfth-century Templars' Rotunda, whose eight columns support an octagonal two-story structure, modeled after the Holy Sepulcher in Jerusalem. The balcony railing of the sixteenth-century nave has inlaid marble supports.

The famous Manueline window of the Convent of Christ, Tomar.

It was in the colonnaded cloister, a masterpiece of sixteenth-century Portuguese architecture built between 1557 and 1566, that tradition says Philip II of Spain declared himself king of Portugal in 1581.

The Manueline window is the main drawing card to the convent. Climb a spiral staircase to reach the Santa Barbara Cloister and the star attraction.

In 1510 at the height of seagoing fervor, Diego de Arrunda, himself possessed and inspired, sculpted a marine fantasy. Coral, seaweed, cork used in ship construction, ropes, anchor chains, cables all burst from the bust of an old sea captain. Two coiled masts are topped with armillary spheres and the whole creation is crowned by the cross of the Order of Christ. The buckled belt to the right is said to be the Order of the Garter, symbolizing the English order presented to Manoel by Henry VII. Its companion, the Order of the Golden Fleece, is to the left.

The convent is open daily (except Christmas) 9:30 A.M.–noon and 2–5 P.M.

Another excursion from Castelo do Bode not to be missed is to Conímbriga, 82 km to the northwest. Highway N-110 north from Tomar winds through olive groves, vineyards, eucalyptus, and pine forest. The village of Penela clings to a hillside crowned by ruins of an eleventh-century castle. From Penela, take the route to Condeixa and after about 16 km, you will see the sign to Conímbriga. Conímbriga can also be reached by bus from Coimbra.

The Coimbrios were of Celtic origin and trod this ancient part of Portugal in the Iron Age. The ruins of Conímbriga, the best-preserved in the country, are those of a Roman city that declined after the arrival of the Suevi in 468.

Near the parking area is a part of the once-important Roman road linking Lisboa and Braga via Tomar. The House of Mosaics contains outstanding designs, especially those showing Perseus tantalizingly dangling the head of Medusa before a sea serpent and droopy Silenus being led along on a donkey.

It is obvious that the Romans used the red soil in the area, because their columns are constructed of red disk-shaped bricks. They also loved their baths—the frigidarium with cold water, the tepidarium with warm, and the caldarium with hot. A drawing of the bath house shows a servant stoking the hypocaust for the solons' comfort.

An aqueduct brought water to activate 457 jets playing gently into a garden fountain. Ask the attendant to demonstrate today's method; a flick of the switch performs the feat electrically. In a museum near the entrance are ceramic and mosaic relics and a few Roman busts.

COIMBRA

There is no pousada in Coimbra and tourist accommodations are meager. But fortunately it may be visited from the pousada in Batalha (82 km), the estalagem in Sangalhos (33 km), or the pousada in Serém (55 km).

According to legend, Coimbra was founded by Hercules in 2000 B.C. Scholars, however, attribute its beginning to the Coimbrios and place the date 1000 years later. It suf-

Shopping day in Coimbra.

fered eons of destruction and reconstruction under the Romans, Visigoths, and Moors until Afonso I established Coimbra as the first capital of Portugal in the twelfth century. King Dinis began the first university in Lisboa in 1290. It was moved to Coimbra twice in the fourteenth century, returned to Lisboa again, where it remained until in 1537 a determined João III established it permanently in his palace in Coimbra.

It may be the historic and artistic monuments that bring visitors to this ancient city, but they will thrill to the pulse and excitement that is Coimbra today. A population of 100,000 lives on hillsides along banks of the Mondego River; jostling through centuries-old narrow streets, one has the feeling that all 100,000 have important business to transact in Cidade Centro. It is best for drivers to park in the first available slot after crossing the Santa Clara Bridge as traffic is horrendous. There is a tourist office near the bridge exit, so pick up a map and plan your walking tour.

To reach the university, board a trolley marked Universidad and in a loud voice say to the conductor, "Universidad, por favor." Then sit back and relax, for not only the driver but fellow passengers will alert you when to debark. Walk toward massive iron gates. Notice the circular mosaic pavement at the entry featuring Minerva, Roman goddess of wisdom and invention.

You enter a large *praça* where the library is found on the left. You must ring for admittance. Tours are sometimes available in English, usually in French. João V built this library of three rooms, one opening onto the other, all lined

You must cross the Santa Clara Bridge for two more stops. Portugal dos Pequeninos is as delightful for adults as for children. Replicas of national monuments and houses typical of Portugal's different regions are built small-scale for children. It is entertaining to watch them duck through doorways, beckoning friends to follow. If one had time, it would be fun to end a tour of Portugal with a visit to Portugal dos Pequeninos to see if all the buildings could be identified.

The other must is a stop at Santa Clara-a-Nova Chapel, facing a large gravel parking lot. Queen Isabel, saintly wife of not-so-saintly King Dinis, is buried in a seventeenth-century silver tomb in a lighted space above the chancel kept supplied with bouquets of fresh flowers. Isabel has the place of honor above the altar. Her statue, carved in wood by Teixeira Lopes, is flanked on the right by a graphic figure of a leper, and on the left by Saint Francis of Assisi. Her original fourteenth-century stone tomb is behind wrought iron screens at the back of the church.

Palace Hotel

BUÇACO, 3050 MEALHADA

***** govt. rating
62 rooms, elevator, gardens
Phone (Mealhada) 93101, 93102
Telex 26349

with 100,000 gold-bound volumes. The dazzle of the books is furthered by gilded Baroque archways. A portrait of the man who also established the great library at Mafra fills the wall at the far end. Ceilings were painted in false perspective to appear vaulted. Along the sides of each room are two writing tables of inlaid rosewood and ebony from Brazil.

The chapel is next door but you can't enter through the Manueline portal. Go through an arch marked Museu and the chapel is to the left. Again you must ring for admittance. The interior has a lovely painted ceiling, seventeenth-century *azulejos*, and a handsome eighteenth-century red and gilt pipe organ.

Once outside again, look beyond the statue of João III commanding the *praça* for a glimpse of the sixteenth-century Sebastião Aqueduct. Opposite João is an ornate building. Go up the stairs to the top-floor office where a guide will conduct you through the Sala dos Capelos. The walls of what was once the great hall of the palace hold portraits of Portuguese kings. The second-floor arcaded gallery that served as vantage point for women today accommodates parents and friends of young students as they are given final oral examinations by doctors of the university.

If you have had your heart set on seeing any of the 14,000 college students wearing the legendary black capes with hems notched after each amorous interlude, you will be disappointed. Coimbra students dress just like students most of the world over --in blue jeans.

In the lower part of town is the Mosteiro de Santa Cruz, reconstructed from a twelfth-century monastery. The interior has eighteenth-century *azulejos* and the magnificently carved tombs of Afonso Henriques, who died in 1135, and of his son Sancho I, who died in 1211.

Enter the upper town through the Arco de Almedina, capped with a tower. This is the last survivor of the medieval town walls. Sé Velha (the old cathedral) is of twelfth-century vintage and is one of the finest Romanesque churches in Portugal. Up above the cathedral is the Machado de Castro Museum, housed in a former bishop's palace. It has a rich treasure including medieval sculptures, religious paintings, period furniture, and an extensive ceramic collection. Roman sculptures and Visigothic artifacts found on the site are displayed in subterranea rooms of the palace.

DIRECTIONS: 30 km north of Coimbra. By car, take the *autostrada* from Coimbra, get off just south of Mealhada, and proceed east a few km to Buçaco.

The Palace Hotel is an elegant, whimsical hodgepodge of Manueline architecture. It was the brainchild of Fernando II, creator of grandiose Pena Palace in Sintra. Ever eager to build something new, he tried to interest his son, King Luis, in a hunting lodge in the Buçaco forest. But Luis's untimely death stifled Fernando's dream.

Several years later, one of King Carlos's ministers came across Fernando's project. He presented it to Carlos, who gave the go-ahead and then apparently forgot all about it. The ambitious minister envisioned more than a mere lodge. His idea was to build a luxury hotel patterned after those on the Riviera. He protected himself, however, by including plans for a private wing just in case Carlos came to call. But the unfortunate king was assassinated before he had the chance and his son, Manoel II, visited only briefly prior to the overthrow of the monarchy in 1910.

Luigi Manini, an Italian, was the architect, and it appears he was determined to outdo Boytac in Manueline embellishment. The arcaded entrance is tiled with *azulejos* painted by Jorge Colaço, depicting scenes from Camões's *Lusiads*. Colaço is also responsible for *The Battle of Ceuta* on walls of the grand staircase, *Cabral's Landing in Brazil*, and to the left of the staircase a tiled wall depicting the first mass celebrated in Brazil. The Battle of Buçaco rages on

Colaço *azulejos* adorn the grand staircase of the Palace Hotel.

the remaining walls of the first-floor grand entrance. Still more artworks upstairs show exploits in Goa, an important former possession of Portugal on the west coast of India.

In the main drawing room, Manini festooned the top of a giant-sized fireplace with a statue of a lute player. A dejected Don Quixote sags across one painted wall of an adjoining salon. Marine murals of mermaids and sea monsters decorate one side of the dining room. Hallways hold priceless Goan furniture and porcelain. Guest room furnishings are from the early twentieth century.

Look for the suit of armor whose eyes light up at night. It's on the first landing of the grand staircase. A circular colonnaded terrace for outside dining overlooks a garden where swans glide on reflective pools.

Fresh flowers are found on each table of the dining room, which is a very popular stop for tour buses, so it is best to make lunch and dinner reservations when registering. The cuisine is outstanding, and wine from the cellar's supply of 200,000 bottles is ever flowing. If you are a label collector, you will be given upon request a new label from Buçaco.

It is a real treat to spend a night or two at the fabulous Palace Hotel. Reservations should be made at least two months in advance.

THE FOREST OF BUCACO. As early as the sixth century, Benedictine monks had constructed rude hermitages in the lush primeval forest of Buçaco. From the eleventh to the sixteenth centuries the woodland was cared for by zealous priests from Coimbra cathedral. Pope Gregory XV issued a decree in 1622 forbidding women entrance to the sylvan sanctuary.

In 1628, the discalced Carmelite order of monks entered the forest and planted many new varieties of trees. They built a monastery and surrounded their realm with an unbroken wall. On the few buildings that Manini did not destroy while building the hotel are mosaic decorations the monks created by breaking up pieces of white quartz, smoky basalt, and rust-colored shale. The insulating capabilities of cork were put to use in beam and wall construction.

Following the dissolution of religious orders in 1834, ownership of the forest passed to the state. Since then the Department of Forestry has planted vegetation procured from distant lands. The forest boasts 400 native varieties of trees and 300 exotic species. After a stroll through the woods, where hydrangeas, magnolias, mimosa, and camellias flourish, one agrees with Suzanne Chantal that "a green cathedral enheld us, and we felt, as in all churches, the cool welcome of silence and peace."

Silence and peace were disturbed in September 1810, when Napoleon's troops were defeated by Wellington's English-Portuguese army on the slopes of Buçaco. Near the hotel is an ancient olive tree under whose branches Wellington is said to have made battle plans. For one week he slept in one of the cells of the monastery while waiting for the French to make the first move.

If the chapel of the former monastery is closed, inquire at the hotel desk and someone will locate the caretaker, who has the keys. Ask to see the painting by Josefa of Obidos (1644), *Our Lady of the Milk,* and notice the unusual ex-votives beneath the painting.

In the military museum located outside forest walls, memorabilia from the Battle of Buçaco is on display. Experts assert that this battle was the beginning of the end of Napoleon.

Pousada São Jerónimo

3475 CARAMULO

B govt. rating
6 rooms, swimming pool
Phone (Viseu) 86291
Telex 53512

DIRECTIONS: 53 km northeast of Buçaco. If driving, at Mortagua turn north onto Highway 228. In the heart of Campo de Besteiros, look for the Pousada sign and turn left toward Caramulo. Pousada São Jerónimo is on the western outskirts of town.

Balconies of the pousada's guest rooms and windows of the dining room take in the verdant Besteiros valley, where *espigueiros,* or granaries, stand out in relief. An apéritif in the pousada's cozy bar is a prelude to dinner by candlelight. House specialties are *borrego assado* (roast lamb), *creme de cebola* (cream of onion soup), *bacalhau com natas* (cod in cream sauce), and *vitela estufada à camponesa* (veal stew). As accompaniment, choose a sparkling Bairrada wine, an Alcobaça *tinto*, or a Torres Vedras *branco*.

On hills above the pousada, framed by the Serra da Estrêla, are dormitories housing people who come to Caramulo for therapeutic mineral baths and pure, brisk air. The town's modern *museu*, faced with slate mined in nearby quarries, has some significant works of art, including originals by Raoul Dufy, Picasso, and Dalí. There are fifteenth-century Portuguese sculptures and a series of colorful tapestries recounting the arrival of the Portuguese in India.

Caramulo boasts another *museu* across the street. The Vintage Car Museum displays 60 shiny automobiles and forerunners of Schwinn bicycles and Harley-Davidson motorcycles. The museums are open daily except Monday 10 A.M.–6 P.M.

The road from Buçaco to Caramulo climbs gradually to an altitude of 2461 feet, offering views of diversified farming. Hillsides are terraced. Grape vines trained on rustic fences form borders of narrow plots planted in corn, squash, *couve galego*, and lettuce. Other strips grow olive, orange, and lemon trees. Intermittent pine forests produce oil and resin. Men collect oil from attached cups, scoop the oozing resin into large containers, and tote the bounty downhill, where it is emptied into tractor-driven tanks.

Estalagem Sangalhos

SANGALHOS

**** govt. rating
30 rooms, swimming pool
Phone 034-74648

DIRECTIONS: 33 km north of Coimbra via N-1. Turn west on Highway 235 and go 2 km.

Twenty rooms of the white, cubistic *estalagem* have outside terrace-balconies. These plus the bar lounge, dining room, and outside dining terrace look down on the lovely Cértima River valley. In the distance are the mountains of Caramulo, Buçaco, and Luso. Guest rooms are attractively furnished with colorful matching bedspreads and drapes.

Specialties of the popular dining room are *carabineiros à la plancha* (grilled shellfish), *bacalhau à nossa moda* (cod served with potatoes and herb mayonnaise), *fondue bourguignonne* (the continental favorite for two people), and *steak au poivre*. House wines are excellent *brancos* and *tintos* from Caves Aliança.

Double room prices include continental breakfast and start at 3300$.

Pousada de Santo António

3750 SEREM

B govt. rating
13 rooms, swimming pool
Phone (Aveiro) 521230
Telex 37150

DIRECTIONS: 50 km north of Coimbra on N-1. The pousada is not difficult to find but it appears, seemingly, from out of nowhere. If driving and approaching on Highway N-1 from the south, look for the Pousada sign and a turn-out on the left when you are ½ km past the end of the bridge over the Vouga River. If approaching from the north, go past signs reading Serém. You will see the pousada sign very shortly. Look for a pink building with a red tiled roof and tall white chimneys perched by itself on a hill.

Santo António was built in the early thirties and was Portugal's first pousada. In 1985 it was remodeled and updated. The setting is serene and the view rewarding. The dining room encompasses bay windows looking out over the Vouga River valley. Garden terraces, vegetable patches, and a swimming pool extend down the slope below the pousada.

If you visit the pousada in autumn you may be lucky enough to be served fresh applesauce with hot, crusty rolls for breakfast. *Sopa de legumes* (vegetable soup) makes a good luncheon or dinner starter. Fish choices range from *lulas grelhadas* (grilled squid) to *sardinhas de escabeche* (pickled sardines). *Fígado grelhado* (grilled liver) is excellent, or select *vitela à Lafões* (roast veal), *carne de porco à regional* (baked pork), or *codornizes fritas* (fried quail). House wines are white and red from Aliança Velho and Borlido Velho wineries and a red Bairrada.

Highway N-230 between Caramulo and Serém affords wonderful rural scenes as the Agueda River tumbles like a mountain stream through steep canyons whose walls are shared by pine trees and agricultural terraces. Occasional ox carts piled with brown forest ferns to serve as winter bedding for farm animals add color to the pastoral picture.

SIDE TRIP FROM SEREM. Aveiro, about 25 km west of Serém, is worth a visit of several hours. It is known as the Venice of Portugal because of crisscrossing canals and hump-backed bridges.

It is believed the Phoenicians were the first to exploit Aveiro's treasure—salt. It remains the primary supplier of Portugal's salt. Geographic location and long hot summers conducive to rapid evaporation produce a fine quality.

In addition to salt production, boat building, and fishing, the harvesting of seaweed, *moliço*, is Aveiro's major industry. When dried and mixed with the debris of crabs, *moliço* makes an excellent fertilizer. Special boats for dragging in tons of *moliço* have evolved. Displaying a Phoenician influence, *moliçeiros* are equipped with long oars, poles to maneuver through shallow water, one sail, large-tined wooden forks for spearing *moliço*, and a very wide rudder. Sweeping upturned prow and stern are painted with colorful scenes or ornamental borders. Somewhere in the design is sure to be found an enlarged eyeball whose significance is obscure.

Follow signs reading Praia (beach) and Porto (harbor) to arrive at the fishing pier. A three-knot current swirls sea water into the network of canals. Lateen sails of entering *moliçeiros* are secured; then the boats are poled into canals. Other traffic consists of barges filled with rocks and salt. The latter are poled into quayside position and unloaded by stouthearted and stoutheaded women and young men carrying reed trays on their heads. Burdened with 100 pounds or so of salt, they trot back and forth conveying their trays into a supply depot serving vessels leaving for distant fishing grounds.

Return to *cidade centro* for a visit to the Convent of Jesus built between the fifteenth and seventeenth centuries. It now houses the Regional Museum. In a church gallery is the marble mosaic tomb of Princess Joana, daughter of Afonso V, who joined the convent in 1472 and died there in 1490. She was canonized near the end of the seventeenth century. The *Portrait of Princess Joana,* painted on wood by Nuno Gonçalves, is one of the convent's prized possessions.

Pousada da Ria

MURTOSA, 3800 AVEIRO

B govt. rating
10 rooms, swimming pool
Phone (Aveiro) 48332
Telex 37061

DIRECTIONS: 38 km northwest of Serém.

Pousada da Ria sits at water's edge facing an extensive lagoon. *Moliceiros* and other small fishing craft make sea-watching interesting and rewarding, especially at sunset. All guest rooms have balconies admitting the sound of lapping waves and the invigorating sea air.

The reception lobby is distinctive. Waterfalls and fountains lead into indoor-outdoor pools where brilliant goldfish swim. Green plants thrive in the atmosphere. Various models of *moliceiros* are displayed on one wall. Leading off from the bar is a lounge facing the water, with comfortable leather furniture grouped around the fireplace. Two green felt–topped game tables are available for cards.

A white marble floor and red leather chairs make an attractive dining room. Unique white coral arrangements and

After the day's harvesting of *moliço*, a *moliceiro* is poled toward the entrance to the canals of Aveiro.

shell collages add decorative touches. Specialties are *caldo verde* (*couve* soup with potatoes and *chouriço* sausage), *caldeirado à ria* (stew of tomatoes, potatoes, eel, and fish), and *robalinhos* (succulent small bass). Two desserts to try are *lait creme* (vanilla custard) and *ovos moles* (egg yolks cooked in boiling sugar). House wines are a Sangalhos *branco* and Bairrada *tinto*, in bottles only.

> *Although Aveiro and Murtosa are not far as the crow flies, they are separated by a two-hour round-trip drive. The entire region from Albergaria-a-Velha westward to Murtosa offers a wealth of sights: teams of oxen, united by vividly painted yokes, pulling carts heaped with* moliço, *seaweed; Gypsies setting up camp in sandy pine groves;* senhoras *nonchalantly balancing trays of turnips on their heads as they stroll along the road; the train mistress halting traffic by holding up a red flag, then cranking barriers into place; families merrily husking corn; young women using a small buck saw on scrap wood; and plate-sized dahlias blooming extravagantly.*

PORTO

Porto, Portugal's second-largest city, is 53 km north of Murtosa. Highway N-1 is a good, fast road.

Before the arrival of the Romans, two small settlements faced one another across the mouth of the Douro River: Portus on the north bank and Cale on the south. Eventually the region stretched northward to the Minho River, came to be known as Portucale, and was the dowry brought by Teresa, daughter of Alfonso VI of Castilla, to Henri of Burgundy. Thus the ancient city bestowed its name on the country.

Three traits have distinguished the citizens of Porto: resistance to outside aggression, self-sacrifice, and love of independence. It is termed the Unconquered City because of fierce opposition to the Moors, to the Spaniards and Philip II, and to the troops of Napoleon. When the fleet was about to embark on the first voyage against Ceuta, the people of Porto contributed the best cuts of meat, saving the least desirable for themselves. This unselfish deed earned them the epithet *tripeiros,* tripe eaters. They evidently developed a taste for tripe because *tripas à moda do Porto* remains a specialty of the city's restaurants.

The strength of Porto's middle class was felt in the early eighteenth century when an edict forbade nobles entrance to city limits. In 1757 the marquis of Pombal tried to prevent English takeover of the wine industry by granting a monopoly to one Portuguese company. Furious lesser wine producers burned down the chosen firm's buildings. In retaliation, Pombal executed 25 arsonists. The spread of republicanism in Portugal was encouraged by the inhabitants of Porto.

"Coimbra sings, Braga prays, Lisboa shows off, and Porto works," goes an old adage. The legendarily brisk pace of life, together with twentieth-century traffic, continues to make Porto hectic and frenzied.

Three remarkable bridges are features of Porto's skyline. Ponte de Dona Maria Pia, a railway bridge, was engineered by the Frenchman Eiffel in 1877. Ponte de Dom Luis was built of iron in 1886 and has two tiers serving both levels of the city on either side of the Douro. Ponta da Arrábida was built in 1963 of reinforced concrete.

Active English interest in the port wine industry for over three centuries is reflected by a British atmosphere in the old part of town. The Methuen Treaty of 1703 provided for England's sale of manufactured goods to Portugal in exchange for wines. Gradually British companies became involved in every phase of wine production, prompting Pombal's ill-fated attempt to establish a Portuguese monopoly.

The exterior of Porto's *sé*, cathedral, begun in the twelfth century, has a fortresslike appearance, but the interior is Baroque. A magnificent silver altar escaped pillage by Napoleon's army when citizens camouflaged it with paint. Walls of the fourteenth-century cloister are covered with scenic *azulejos*.

The Church of São Francisco, Portugal's most ornate church, has an interior of opulent gold leaf.

The Palácio da Bolsa (stock exchange), built in the nineteenth century, has a statue-bedecked marble grand staircase and the Arabian hall, lavish with stained glass windows and Alhambra-like decorative stucco work.

For a panoramic view of Porto and the Douro valley, go to the top of the 246-foot Clérigos Tower adjacent to the eighteenth-century Church of the Clérigos.

Take a cab to Vila Nova de Gaia on the south bank of the Douro. Here are the wine lodges, where port is stored in immense vats. The main lodges are open for wine tasting on weekdays. By sampling a few varieties, one acquires an appreciation of Portugal's world-famous alcoholic beverage.

In Porto's São Bento railroad station, see pictorial *azulejos* recounting episodes from the life of Afonso Henriques.

Pousada Santa Maria da Oliveira

4800 GUIMARAES

C govt. rating
16 rooms
Phone 412157
Telex 32875

DIRECTIONS: 49 km northeast of Porto. If driving, follow signs through constricted streets to the pousada parking "lot." Walk around and past the dining room with French windows to enter under a circular wrought iron hanging Pousada sign.

A few years ago the city government bought up several sixteenth-century houses on Rua Santa Maria, built a new residential complex for the displaced persons, and converted their former homes into a stunning pousada. This is one of two pousadas owned by local rather than national government.

Guest rooms are beautifully decorated with matching linen drapes, bedspreads, carpets, and embroidered lamp shades. There is a comfortable TV room and two open areas serving as a bar. All public rooms show the hand of an expert decorator in the number of unique and interesting objets d'art on tables and walls. Displayed local handcraft is for sale.

The dining room is very popular both for its marvelous view of Largo da Oliveira, an attractive square, and for its cuisine. Minho *vinhos verdes* and rosés enhance such entrees as *filetes de pescada recheados* (filets of whiting), *coelho estufado* (rabbit stew), and *rolinhos de linguado com laranja* (rolls of sole with orange).

TOURING GUIMARAES. Largo da Oliveira is fronted by Colegiada de Nossa Senhora da Oliveira, founded in the tenth century by Galician Countess Mumadona, whose statue has a place of honor in a *praça* of the town. The ancient church has undergone several reconstructions over the centuries. The name, meaning Our Lady of the Olive Tree, derives from two legends. One says that when Wamba, a Visigothic farmer, was selected king in 672, he was so reluctant that he plunged his staff into the earth swearing he would not accept unless his staff sprouted olive branches, which of course it did—immediately. Another legend goes that as the stone gazebo, a memorial to the victory over the Moors in the Battle of Salado, was being completed in 1343, the trunk of an olive tree in front of the church suddenly sprouted leaves.

The Museu Alberto Sampaio is housed in church buildings surrounding a cloister rebuilt by João I. In addition to collections of ceramics, paintings, and sculpture, there are two historical items to see: the tunic worn by João at the Battle of Aljubarotta and a silver triptych of Juan I of Castilla said to have been seized from the Spanish king during the battle and presented to João.

Another worthwhile museum to visit is that of archeologist Martins Sarmento, who began excavating ancient *citânias* in 1875. On display are collections of Roman altars, inscribed stones, sarcophaguses, bronze artifacts, coins, and the Pedra Formosa, a large yoke-shaped stone thought to have been the front part of a mausoleum. Try to visit this museum after you have seen Citânia de Briteiros for a better appreciation of the way of life.

Guimarães is called the Cradle of Portugal because it was the birthplace of the first king, Afonso Henriques. He was born in the 79-foot-high keep of a tenth-century castle erected by his father, Henri of Burgundy. In the fifteenth century, seven square towers on bedrock were added as further protection. Rewarding views of the area are had by walking along the ramparts.

Just down the hill is the small twelfth-century Romanesque Church of São Miguel do Castelo, where Afonso is believed to have been baptized. Ask for the chapel key at the Paço dos Duques, palace of the dukes of Bragança, built in the fifteenth century but deserted 100 years later when the Braganças moved to Vila Viçosa. The palace was reconstructed during the Salazar era to serve as his official residence in northern Portugal. There are priceless pieces of antique furniture, tapestries, porcelains, and canvases by Josefa of Obidos. Is it possible that the hideous red brick chimneys are original? A handsome bronze statue of Afonso Henriques near the entrance to the palace looks more authentic.

SIDE TRIPS FROM GUIMARAES. If it's Thursday or close to it, plan on going to Barcelos, 40 km northwest. It is no exaggeration to say that a trip to Portugal should be planned with Barcelos's Thursday market in mind.

The *mercado* has two locations and both must be visited.

Heading for the meat market in Barcelos.

The trick is to find the place whence come streams of shoppers whose heads and hands carry the morning's purchases. If driving, proceed up a hill to a large, nondescript concrete building. Squeeze into a parking spot, and head toward the action.

First-floor stalls, open to a center patio, are kept supplied by bustling women bearing trays of fish on their heads. They manage this incredible feat, seen throughout Portugal, by first securing to their pates a flat "doughnut." Then with a swift hoist, they position their burden. Moving off rapidly, they achieve balance by a barely perceptible side to side motion of their heads. Wonderful to see.

On the way to the upstairs balcony of shops, you may

be beckoned to a pile of women's panties heaped on the floor and encouraged to purchase a nylon triangle by a laughing *senhora*. After a tour of meat, poultry, fruit, and vegetable stalls, head downhill and locate Campo da República.

In this tree-lined area equal to four square blocks, small pathways radiate from a central stone fountain. No space is wasted as vendors sell grain, potatoes, and onions in bulk, delicious Portuguese bread in many shapes and sizes, cheeses, clothing, dishes, pots and pans, barrels, bric-a-brac, hand-carved wooden shovels and ox yokes, and crude regional pottery. Smoke from braziers roasting chestnuts around the fountain curls through the air.

Barcelos is the birthplace of the story of what seems to be the country's mascot—the rooster. It is similar to Spain's folktale of the cock.

It seems that during the Middle Ages an evil crime was committed in Barcelos. It remained unsolved until the day a suspicious-looking Galician appeared in town. He was accused of the crime. Denying his guilt, he protested that he was on pilgrimage to São Tiago de Compostela to fulfill a vow made to Saint James. But all protestations were in vain for he was condemned to be hanged. Granted his last request, he was taken before the magistrate who had pronounced sentence.

The judge, at dinner with friends, was about to partake of succulent roast chicken. The desperate Galician pleaded, "As surely as I am innocent will that cock crow if I am hanged!" The unfortunate man was dragged to the gallows and the noose placed round his neck, whereupon the cock on the judge's platter rose to full height and crowed lustily.

The already dangling victim was saved just in time by the distraught judge, who rushed to the scene. It is said that years later the Galician returned to Barcelos and erected a monument to Saint James. An interesting relic in the town's archeological museum, which is installed in ruins of the former palace of the ducal counts of Barcelos, is the fourteenth-century memorial to the cock who had saved the life of the Galician pilgrim. The site of the original ducal palace was given by João I to Nuno Alvares Pereira in gratitude for his triumph at the Battle of Aljubarrota.

There are two sights to see near Braga, 22 km north of Guimarães. Braga was known as Bracara Augusta to the Romans. The Suevi invading in the fifth century made the town their capital. Braga passed next to the Visigoths, then to the Moors, and after the Reconquest, gained prominence as the religious heart of the country. In the Capela dos Reis (kings' chapel) of Braga's *sé* (cathedral), rebuilt in the twelfth century on 300-year-old foundations, are the tombs of Teresa and Henri of Burgundy and the mummified remains of the archbishop of Braga, who participated in the Battle of Aljubarrota.

Bom Jesus do Monte (good Jesus of the mount) is a Joanine church built in the late eighteenth century and located 4 km from Braga. You can either drive to the church's lofty location or park below and walk the Holy Way up the Stairway of the Five Senses. This pilgrims' path is lined with small chapels, each containing a scene from the Passion with lifesize and lifelike figures. Flower beds pave the approach to the church. For a restful lunch or apéritif, stop in at the Hotel do Elevador, whose dining room offers a remarkable panorama of Braga and environs.

The ruins of Citânia de Briteiros are a few kilometers to the east of Braga and stand at an altitude of 1102 feet. Markers point the way—in Portuguese—through the settlement, which was in existence from the eighth to the fourth centuries B.C. Don't despair of finding the two reconstructed stone huts. Keep trudging up and around until you reach the summit. Discoveries unearthed by Sarmento are found in the museum in Guimarães.

Pousada de Santa Marinha da Costa

PENHA
4800 GUIMARAES

CH govt. rating
60 rooms, gardens
Phone 418453
Telex 32686

DIRECTIONS: The pousada is in the Penha National Park a few kilometers southeast of Guimarães.

Opened in 1985, the pousada was reconstructed from a monastery founded in 1154, and is surrounded by lovely gardens. The monastery church, begun in 1748, is decorated with *azulejos* by Policapo de Oliveira Bernardes.

Interesting entrees are *pescada da póvoa com vinho do Porto* (whiting with port wine sauce), *bacalhau com broa de milho e cerveja* (cod cooked in beer with maize bread), *trutas à moda do Minho* (fresh trout), *mexilhões à convento* (mussels), *filetes de solha com camarão* (fish filets with shrimp), and *vitela entronchada* (veal steak with cabbage). Soups include *sopa de grão com espinafres* (chickpea with spinach), *puré de ervilhas* (cream of pea), and *sopa de feijão encarnado com couve lombarda* (red bean soup with cabbage).

Hotel Santa Luzia
4900 VIANA DO CASTELO

**** govt. rating
60 rooms, swimming pool, tennis
Phone 22192

DIRECTIONS: 79 km northwest of Guimarães. Approaching Viana do Castelo from the south, you will see the Hotel de Santa Luzia, a large white bulding, at the top of a hill. After crossing the Lima River, follow signs reading Santa Luzia. You will pass the Basilica de Santa Luzia just before reaching the lofty hotel.

The hotel began life as a palace in the late nineteenth century. Fifty years later, two additional stories completed its conversion into a resort facility.

Spacious salons are illuminated by crystal chandeliers. Two circular rooms extend from both ends of the first floor. One is a card room, the other an alcove off the dining room. On one wall of the main salon hangs a modern tapestry depicting the terror of Roman legions about to cross what they believed to be the River of Forgetfulness, the Lima.

TOURING VIANA DO CASTELO. On a knoll facing the hotel entrance are ruins of a *citânia*. It is eerie exploring the prehistoric village. Dwellings here were 15 feet in diameter; entry stones were laid in a diagonal pattern.

The Basilica de Santa Luzia is in the Byzantine style. In its rather small interior are three beautiful stained glass windows, a glittering chandelier, and fine-toned bells that ring on the quarter hour. A belvedere extending from steps of the basilica presents a spectacular scene of the old town, the estuary of the Lima, and the Atlantic breaking on the shore.

Viana was founded in 1258 following a grant from Afonso III. It grew from a small fishing community to eminence as Portugal's second port. But gradual silting of the harbor and decline of the country's prosperity led to its deterioration.

In the eighteenth century, gold and diamonds from Brazil pumped new life into Portugal and thence into Viana. Most of the town's Baroque churches and buildings date from that era. It was Queen Maria II who dignified its name with the addition of do Castelo.

The Minho region's colorful folklore may be seen during the third week of August. Romaria Nossa Senhora da Agonia, festival of Our Lady of Sorrow, includes a farm animal fair, bullfights, folk music and dancing, parades in traditional costumes, a procession to the sea organized by fishermen, and fireworks. Secular festivities end with a religious march to the Church of Nossa Senhora da Agonia.

Caminha, 21 km north of Viana, is a serene fishing hamlet whose fortifications attest to former military importance. Plan to have lunch here. On the central square edged with seventeenth-century houses, locate the clock tower. Go down a narrow street behind the tower to the Caminhense, a small restaurant where gourmet food is prepared by owner Manuel, who is Portuguese, and served by his German wife, Lisa. Both speak fluent English, making for a delightful luncheon hour.

Pousada de Dom Dinis

4920 VILA NOVA DE CERVEIRA

CH govt. rating
29 rooms
Phone (Valença) 95601
Telex 32821

DIRECTIONS: 39 km northeast of Viana do Castelo on N-13.

Vila Nova is a small town that comes alive on market day. Otherwise there is not much activity. Pousada de Dom Dinis, named for the monarch who in 1321 granted a charter to a castle and its inhabitants on the town site, was opened in 1982. It has an unusual setting. The reception office is found across the street from an 1809 war monument, up a few hundred yards from the church. After registering, you take your luggage up through castle walls along a cobbled path to one of three buildings reconstructed from ancient castle dwellings.

Carpeted guest rooms are quite large, having a desk, occasional chairs, and tall beds with ornately carved central paneled headboards. The bar-lounge is in a separate building at the summit of the cobbled walkway.

The dining room is in still another building beyond a terrace for outside dining. Window walls of the modern dining hall look out to the Minho River and surrounding valleys. Food is exceptional. Specialties are *trutas à minhota* (fresh trout from the Minho River), *pato assado com arroz* (roast duck with rice), and *cerdo assado,* our favorite. Pineapple slices, french fries, baked tomato, and cauliflower accompany the roast pork. *Tarta de maçã* (apple tart) makes a satisfying dessert. Dining hours are 12:30–2:30 P.M. and 7:30–9:30 P.M.

Estalagem da Boega
GONDAREM, 4920 VILA NOVA
DE CERVEIRA

40 rooms, gardens, tennis courts,
    swimming pool

DIRECTIONS: 4 km south of Vila Nova de Cerveira. Leave the highway at the Estalagem sign and proceed for a block or two. Then follow a very narrow road under a grape arbor and head for a large white building on a low hill.

The main part of the *estalagem* is the large white building, a convent in the seventeenth century. There are additional rooms in a new motel-type annex off to the left. Breakfast is included in room prices, which are 2500 escudos for a

double in the old section, 2200 escudos for the new annex, and 2900 escudos for a suite. There is no menu in the *azulejo*-wainscoted dining room. Guests are obliged to take the day's offerings, but delicious odors emanating from the kitchen seemed to promise a tasty meal. Lunch and dinner cost 800 escudos each. Be sure to peek into the small chapel, whose walls are completely covered with *azulejos*.

Pousada de São Teotónio

4930 VALENCA DO MINHO

C govt. rating
22 rooms, gardens
Phone 22252
Telex 32837

DIRECTIONS: 53 km northeast of Viana do Castelo.

Advance reservations at Valença's pousada are recommended because of its popularity with Portuguese as well as foreign tourists. On Spain's holiday weekends, crossing the international bridge into Portugal can take hours and conditions at the border bank are hectic. At those times the streets of Valença are jammed with Spaniards buying excellent, inexpensive Portuguese products. Therefore if possible, plan a stay here during the week.

The pousada sits at the end of the main street and has all the attributes of a comfortable, successful inn. Public and guest rooms are graciously furnished and have windows opening to a spectacular vista. Beyond ramparts of a seventeenth-century fort, the placid Minho River flows through a lush valley extending to hills of the ancient township of Tuy framed by the mountains of Galicia.

Bacalhau à pousada (cod baked in a savory sauce), *rojões de porco à minhota* (pork tenderloin), and *salmão do rio Minho* (fresh salmon from the Minho) are pousada specialties. *Sobremesas* include a meringue confection, an orange-flavored gelatin, and a coconut sweet topped with frosting. House wines are reds and whites from Adegas Ponte de Lima and Ponte da Barca. Alvarinho is a light dry *branco*.

VALENÇA DO MINHO AND ENVIRONS. To reach the town of Valença, drive through three gateways of the old fort, which was once surrounded by double ramparts and two moats. Although such fortifications, with the cannon still in place, look impregnable, the town was taken twice—once by Castilians during the days of Afonso III and again in 1834 by British Admiral Napier acting in behalf of Pedro IV in struggles against his brother, Miguel.

The third gateway leads into the village, where iron lanterns extend over cobbled streets edged with shops selling sweaters, table linens, ceramic ware, and other handcrafts.

A two-day visit at this pleasant pousada allows time for shopping in Valença and for a trek over the international bridge. A word of advice: Stop at the border bank and get pesetas because neither escudos nor dollars are accepted in Spanish establishments. It is frustrating not to be able to slake a thirst or purchase a souvenir.

In autumn, on the 18-km drive along the Minho from Valença to Monção, blue hydrangeas, russet grape leaves, and yellow sycamores color a landscape of forests and fields broken by pyramidal corn stalks and clusters of farmhouses. A different breed of cattle appears, *gado barrosão*. Widespread horns curve gracefully upward and huge brown eyes are fringed by thick curly lashes.

Monção is another fortified town now resting at peace on the banks of the Minho. Here a story is told about the heroism and ingenuity of a mayor's wife who once saved the town by daily furnishing bread to attackers, leading them to conclude that their siege was in vain.

Casa de Roda

4950 MONCAO

Phone 52105

DIRECTIONS: about 18 km east of Valença.

As we mentioned in the introduction, it takes a lot of time to locate Portugal's *solares,* or manor houses, because signs are nonexistent and directions sent from the tourist offices are not precise. However, we did locate two.

Casa de Roda is owned by Senhora Maria Luisa-Távora. Open wrought iron gates to the entrance doorway and pull a string, ringing a bell for admittance.

Built in the sixteenth century, the *solar* was gutted by fire during a war with the Spanish, then rebuilt in the eighteenth century. Rooms hold antique furniture, bric-a-brac, paintings, and etchings. Two double rooms with sparkling, tiled attached baths have been attractively furnished for guests. Only breakfast is served.

Heading south from Monção, you soon pass a fabulous Manueline palace on the right. The estate is walled and the entrance guarded by high iron gates but a glimpse is possible. It is the Palácio de Brejoeira, with 50 acres planted in Alvarinho grapes. The adjoining winery produces a high-quality, very pale, fruity dry wine. It is rather expensive but well worth the extra escudos.

Casa do Barreiro

4990 PONTE DE LIMA

Swimming pool
Phone 941627

DIRECTIONS: East of Viana do Castelo on Highway 203. 4 km past
Ponte de Lima you will see the *casa* on the left.

In the area around Ponte de Lima and Ponte da Barca there
are several *solares*. Casa do Barreiro is easy to find, but you
come upon it suddenly.

   Owned by Senhor Gaspar Malheiro, the *solar* was built
in the seventeenth century. The main house can accommodate five guests in two doubles and one single room
(all with baths). Beyond a large courtyard with a fountain
in the center, is an annex housing eight more guests. There
is a small bar off the living room, a TV room, and a dining
room. Price per couple is 3000 escudos per night, breakfast, lunch, or dinner included.

   The casa has lovely *azulejos* on outside walls and around
fountains.

Pousada de São Bento

CANICADA, 4850 VIEIRA
DO MINHO

C govt. rating
10 rooms, swimming pool
Phone (Braga) 57190
Telex 32339

DIRECTIONS: 35 km northeast of Braga.

Pousada de São Bento overlooks a *barragem*, dam, con-structed to hold water from the Cávado River. Peneda-Gerês National Park, created in 1970 for the preservation of regional flora and fauna, extends for miles across the Cávado and furnishes rich views of nature from the lounge and dining room of the São Bento.

Guest rooms are small and have low ceilings but there are adequate "escape hatches" for reading and relaxation. In the unusual common area, one large room is open to salon and dining area. Both share a centrally located fireplace. Side balconies on two sides of the high-ceilinged room offer additional clusters of seating. Trailing plants fall in profusion over balcony railings. A heavy gilt chandelier hangs from rafters of the vaulted ceiling.

Small lanterns on each dining table emit soft light from tiny nail-hole openings. The food is excellent. Select from entrees such as *lombo à "Salsicheiro"* (pork cutlets), *trutas à la bordalesa* (fresh trout with Bordelaise sauce), or *rins com cogumelos* (kidney with mushrooms). Be sure to order *torta de maçã*, a delicious apple tart.

If arriving at Caniçada from Braga, follow signs to Chaves. The road goes through one small town after another. Herds of goats are tended by young boys who whistle instructions and warnings to their animals. Men can be seen playing a Portuguese version of horseshoes. In this area, grape vines are trained around trunks of olive and taller trees so that pickers do their chores from ladders. Olive trunks also support stalks of drying corn. Near Caniçada, in autumn, young maple trees spark forests with brilliant red. When you've gone 30 km from Braga, watch for the familiar Pousada sign and make a left turn off the highway.

Pousada de São Gonçalo

4600 AMARANTE

B govt. rating
17 rooms
Phone (Penafiel) 461113
Telex 26321

DIRECTIONS: 58 km southeast of Guimarães. Coming from Guimarães, follow signs to Vila Real. The first Pousada sign appears on the southern outskirts of Amarante. The remaining 24 km are over a very winding road where top speed is about 35 km per hour.

Pousada de São Gonçalo sits alone on a ledge overlooking the Tâmega valley, which is almost enclosed by the granite Serra do Marão. Guest rooms are quite small but the circular bar and dining room are appealing and offer views of a lonely, interesting countryside.

Food specialties include *creme de espargos* (cream of asparagus soup), *frango com arroz* (stewed chicken with rice), *trutas recheadas com presunto* (trout stuffed with ham), *lombo de porco assado com espinafres* (roast pork with spinach), and *peru assado* (roast turkey). With any of these entrees, order either a sparkling Lamego wine or an Amarante *vinho verde*.

AMARANTE AND ENVIRONS. Amarante's centuries-old houses stairstep both banks of the Tâmega River and are joined by a low-arched granite bridge constructed in the late eighteenth century. This landmark of Amarante is a national monument and a plaque at the left-bank entrance honors its successful defense against French troops in 1809.

São Gonçalo was a Dominican priest who lived as a hermit yet curiously became the town's patron saint of marriage. His thirteenth-century bridge served the village until it was replaced by the present *ponte*. São Gonçalo died in 1259 and his tomb rests in a sixteenth-century monastery bearing his name.

Amarante is famous for its *vinho verde* and its pastries with unusual names which are baked in phallic shapes. The feast day of São Gonçalo is celebrated on the first Saturday in June.

The mountains west of the pousada are desolate, suited only for the hardy goats who scamper over forbidding terrain.

The descent from the pousada east to Vila Real is not so harsh. Small villages of slate-roofed houses with their accompanying tiny plots of terraced corn are scattered on the rocky slopes. Along the road, local artisans sell their distinctive black pottery.

Vila Real is some 27 km east of the pousada. The largest town in the region of Trás-os-Montes (meaning "beyond the mountains"), it was granted a charter by Afonso III in 1272. Vila Real is the scene of great activity when Saint Peter's Fair is held every June 29.

Take Highway 322 east from Vila Real for 2 km to Sabrosa. When signs indicate Solar de Mateus, turn into wooded grounds for a sight familiar to wine lovers—Palácio de Mateus, whose picture is displayed on bottles of Mateus wine.

Built by Nicolau Nasone for António José Botelho Mourão in 1739, the *solar* is a perfect example of Portuguese Baroque architecture. Patterned flower beds, rows of clipped hedges, and shimmering pools surround the mansion. The owner's name is Dom Francisco de Sousa Botelho de Alburquerque, count of Mangualde, fourth count of Vila Real, and count of Mello. He keeps the *solar* open for touring and for cultural events.

Solar de Mateus, Vila Real

Nearby is SOGRAPE winery, which pays for use of the name and picture of the Mateus mansion. The free guided tour takes in all processes of wine production in an efficient, impressively sterile facility where 250,000 liters are bottled daily. The firm's yearly production is exported to 120 countries, between 30 percent and 40 percent being shipped to the United States. Complimentary glasses of chilled Mateus are served in the company's hospitality room at the end of the one-hour tour.

Golfers may want to check out the 9-hole, par 36 course in Vidago, 50 km north of Vila Real.

Pousada Barão de Forrester

5070 ALIJO

B govt. rating
11 rooms, garden
Phone (Vila Real) 95215, 95304
Telex 26364

DIRECTIONS: 56 km east of Vila Real. There is no sign announcing the pousada; if entering town from Lamego or Vila Real, turn right at the Y in the road and you are there. The two-story white building with granite-framed windows and red-tiled roof is a typical Portuguese country home. The *correio* (post office) is the next building. Drive through black iron gates, park in the rear and ring for entrance.

The pousada was named for James Forrester, a Scot who opened the Douro River to navigation and was dubbed *barão* (baron) by a grateful Fernando II. On a pousada wall hangs a map of the wine district of the upper Douro drawn by Forrester in 1842. The outspoken wine expert was drowned in rapids of the Douro in 1861.

Guest rooms have twin beds with matching bedspreads and drapes. Windows look out over countryside brimming with vines. Walls of the cozy TV lounge are decorated with a hand-painted mural on a vine theme. There are two dining areas, one inside and the other used as a terrace during warm weather. The colorful decor in both rooms leaves visitors with no doubt that they are in wine country.

A typical *ementa do dia* offers *sopa de legumes* (vegetable soup) or *ovos mexidos com tomate* (scrambed eggs with tomato), *bacalhau à Barão de Forrester* (cod), or *filetes de pescada com maionese* (filets of hake with a mayonnaise sauce). Third-course choices are *iscas de fígado à portuguesa* (braised liver) or *entrecosto de vitela grelhado* (grilled veal steak). Fruit, a sweet, or local cheese comes next. With dinner enjoy a Dão *tinto* from Grão Vasco and after dinner a superior tawny port bottled for the pousada.

The pousada is so charming and the staff so friendly that it is to be hoped that it will remain open to serve tourists exploring this fascinating part of Portugal. Like the pousada in Guimarães, the establishment is owned by the town council, sometimes at odds with ENATUR, who manages the place. It would be wise to check beforehand about the pousada's status rather than take a chance.

ENVIRONS. Exploring the area east of Vila Real on secondary roads yields marvelous sights. Oxen pulling heavy carts have a thick leather "pudding" above their eyes to protect their heads and necks as they strain with their burdens. In autumn, whole families are busy picking grapes. Grapes in plastic sacks are stacked atop low stone walls. Others are heaped in large primitive baskets set alongside the road. All are awaiting pick-up by the cooperative. If it's Sunday, hunters are out with their hounds, braces of quail hanging over their shoulders.

The ideal time to visit Trás-os-Montes is around the middle of October, when the days are still fairly warm and the nights cool. This is the time of the grape harvest, with exciting activities and sights. Just down the street from Pousada Barão de Forrester is the town wine cooperative. Farmers bring in their barrels of grapes either in trucks or on horse or donkey carts. Preference in line is given to animal-powered vehicles. A probe is lowered into the container of grapes and about a quart of juice is extracted. This sample is then taken to an adjacent small building for sugar analysis. The more sugar, the better the quality of wine. The farmer is given a slip of paper showing the sugar count. All will share proportionately in the cooperative's profits. All grapes here are used to make port and muscatel.

Estalagem de Caçador

MACEDO DE CAVALEIROS, 5340
BRAGANCA

25 rooms, swimming pool, elevator
Phone 42356

DIRECTIONS: 100 km northeast of Alijó.

For those making further excursions into a comparatively little-known area of Portugal, a very pleasant experience awaits at Estalagem de Caçador (hunter). Once the town hall, built in the mid-1800s, the inn is owned by family members of the Quinta de Valpredinhos, whose vineyards supply the estalagem with exceptional wines. Dona Maria Manuela is the gracious manager and host.

The entry hall and large lounge are decorated with hunting memorabilia. The coat rack sprouts goats' hooves. Elephant tusks and cases of stuffed birds are on display. Guest rooms are furnished with antique furniture, Arraiolos area rugs, eiderdown comforters, and crochet-trimmed bedspreads. One single room has a carved headboard from 1846 and rich velvet drapes. Each room is decorated differently and achieves the aim of seeming more like a private home than a hotel. Marble-floored hallways hold cases of various collections: mugs and pitchers, glass and porcelain shoes, and Barcelos pottery.

In the dining room, silverware is turned upside down because the monogram is on the back. Two delectables to order are *bacalhau bolos* (french-fried codfish balls) and *molotov*, an outstanding dessert made by folding burnt sugar into egg whites. The meringue·is then baked slowly and when done, topped with an egg yolk custard.

Price of a double room is 3300 escudos. Meals begin at 800 escudos. Picnic lunches can be made to order for guests wanting to explore neighboring villages. Macedo's market days are the sixth, eighteenth, and twenty-ninth of each month.

ENVIRONS. The road from Alijó to Macedo goes through Vila Flor, another vinicultural center that boasts two Roman fountains plus the gate through which Dom Dinis once came to call. Saturday is market day in Mirendela, whose medieval bridge of 17 arches spans the River Tua.

In this part of Trás-os-Montes, there is a special sausage, *alheira*, which everyone makes differently. The story goes that it was to this region that many Jews fled Inquisitions in Spain and Portugal. Though they became "new" Christians, their sausage never contained pork. Today's *alheiras* are made with bread crumbs, spices, chicken, veal, rabbit, and still no pork.

In the early part of this century, Clemente Meneres, a Porto exporter of cork and olive oil, came riding into the town of Romeu (7 km northeast of Mirandela) on horseback one rainy night. He needed food and a bed. He was taken in by Maria Rita, who despite being desperately poor cooked him such an incomparable meal that he decided to do something about the town's situation. After taking stock, he bought Romeu and two adjoining towns, had the homes repaired, electrified all three towns, and saw to it that every inhabitant had a bed.

The hamlet of Romeu has a restaurant, the Maria Rita, open daily except Monday noon–10 p.m., and a museum, Loja das Curiosidades. Made up of Meneres's personal collection, the museum exhibits old cars, typewriters, sewing machines, and music boxes.

Pousada
de São Bartolomeu
5300 BRAGANCA

B govt. rating
22 rooms
Phone 22493
Telex 22613

DIRECTIONS: 135 km northeast of Vila Real, 42 km northeast of Macedo de Cavaleiros. Approaching Bragança from the west or south, you will see the Pousada sign before entering the town proper. Follow its direction up a hill across a ravine from the walled town and castle.

Guest rooms of Pousada de São Bartolomeu are large enough to accommodate twin beds, two occasional chairs, and a desk alcove. Balcony views take in the twelfth-century castle, old town, and extensive new suburbs to the north. Comfortable seating groups are arranged before a stone fireplace in the lounge-bar.

Two interesting soups appear on the pousada menu: *sopa de agriões* (watercress soup) and *creme de cenoura* (cream of carrot). Ensuing entrees could be *medalhões de vitela grelhados* (grilled medallions of veal), *bacalhau dourado* (fried cod), or *lombo de porco grelhado à modo de Bragança* (grilled pork chops).

BRAGANCA AND ENVIRONS. In 1387 John of Gaunt and son-in-law João I passed through Bragança, ancient capital of Trás-os-Montes. They spent the night at the castle, built in 1187 by Sancho I, with a square keep protected by several watchtowers. Massive stone walls enclose the old town clustered around the castle. It became the property of the house of Bragança in 1442 when the title duke of Bragança was created for Dom Afonso, natural son of João I. The Bragança family ruled Portugal from 1640 to 1910. In the mid-1800s, the title of duke of Bragança was bestowed on the heir to the throne, a tradition that lasted until 1910.

Adjacent to and a little behind sixteenth-century St. Mary's Church is Domus Municipalis, the oldest town hall in the country. Built in the twelfth century, the five-sided structure has a vaulted roof and round open arches on each side. A grille in the rough stone floor covers the town's old cistern.

The drive from Vila Real to Bragança on Highway 15 will take about three and a half hours. Sheep graze on bleak land that somehow manages to yield corn in small patches. Sections of planted forests give way to a region where tiny parcels of grapes and corn are walled with the same kind of stones used in construction of local houses. Approaching Murça, the winding road passes through barren fields broken by rocky outcrops. Extraordinary terracing has been achieved and the meager soil has been coaxed to support olive trees and grapes.

The *porca* of Murça is seen from the highway. Its origin is disputed. Some say the stone boar is a relic from the Iron Age; others believe it was fashioned in the seventh century in celebration of a landowner's killing of a wild boar that had menaced the community.

The landscape is seldom monotonous as it changes from gentle hillocks to fields of wheat and groves of cork, olive, almond, and chestnut trees. At occasional roadside stands, you can buy *queijo* (cheese, pronounced KAY-zhoo) made from ewes' or goats' milk and sacks of almonds, twice as large as the ones seen in the U.S. and difficult to crack.

Pousada de Santa Catarina

5210 MIRANDA DO DOURO

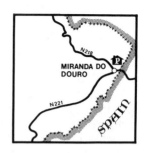

B govt. rating
12 rooms
Phone (Bragança) 42255

DIRECTIONS: 83 km southeast of Bragança. When approaching from Bragança, at the top of the hill where a sign reads Miranda do Douro, drive straight ahead to reach Pousada de Santa Catarina.

Guest and public rooms face a rocky canyon, the sapphire waters of the Douro River, and a dam. For a change of pace, begin a meal in the pousada dining room with *creme de abóbora* (cream of pumpkin soup). Follow that with *favas à transmontana* (bean stew flavored with sausage), *escalopes panados com arroz de tomate* (beef chops with tomato rice), or *ensopado de polvo* (a stew featuring octopus).

MIRANDA DO DOURO AND ENVIRONS. Henri of Burgundy, father of Afonso I, drove the Moors from Miranda's castle. In 1286 King Dinis rebuilt the ramparts because he was quarreling in warlike fashion with Alfonso IX of León. Dinis became so protective of Miranda that he vowed it would never pass from the crown of Portugal. The city's frontier importance was realized by Fernando I, who minted coins displaying the "fez" of Miranda. In 1510, after Manoel I gave his blessings, it became an important commercial center.

Miranda reached full status when Pope Paul III, encouraged by João III, authorized the creation of a diocese and the resultant cathedral was started in 1545. However, during the reign of Maria I, Pope Pius VI revoked the privilege and passed the diocese to Bragança. That is why Miranda's religious edifice is called *igreja* (church), not *sé* (cathedral).

A canyon cut by the Douro River forms a natural boundary between Spain and Portugal. The two countries have constructed a series of five dams, Miranda being the first.

Make an effort to see *O Menino Jesus da Cartolinha* in Santa Maria Church. A naive carved wooden statue of the "boy Jesus" is kept in an enclosed glass case. He sports a top hat and is surrounded by an extensive wardrobe. On days of special religious observance, he is lovingly dressed in the appropriate attire.

Toward the end of the first week in September, Miranda has a great fair. Regional folk dances are performed. In the famed Pauliteiros Dance, men wearing colorful costumes perform rhythmic dances, brandishing swordlike sticks called *paulitos*.

The residents of Miranda speak the only dialect found in Portugal, called Mirandês, but tourists should have no problem communicating.

If heading south, leave the pousada in Miranda by the same route of entry and follow the sign to Mogadouro. Highway 221 is a good road where a speed of 100 kilometers per hour can be maintained. However, be alert for sheep and cattle crossings. The air is dry and fresh, the countryside gently rolling wheat fields.

In autumn, hillsides are afire with grape leaves. Sudden granite "whales" disrupt plowed fields. What traffic there is consists of an occasional tractor, motorcycle, oxcart, or burro. Patches of emerald lettuce grow on the outskirts of Mogadouro, where castle ruins remain in view as the road starts to climb through hillocks furry with newly planted pine trees.

South of Mogadouro there is no vegetation for a stretch of several kilometers. Apple orchards provide a brief respite in the vicinity of Figueira de Castelo Rodrigo, whose timeless fortress remnants crown a rugged mountain.

Pousada de Almeida

ALMEIDA

CH govt. rating
21 rooms

DIRECTIONS: 17 km north of Vilar Formoso (on international border near Ciudad Rodrigo, Spain).

The new pousada is scheduled for completion and inauguration by the summer of 1986. Built within walls of the ancient city, the pousada's rooms will have baths, and there will be public lounges and a restaurant.

Almeida has always been in a vulnerable position because of its proximity to Spain. A hill 2500 feet high was chosen for fortification. After the Reconquest, King Dinis gave the town a charter and repaired the bastion. In 1510 Manoel strengthened Almeida's position because the walls had been penetrated by Enrique of Trastamara in 1373 and a few years later by Juan I. In the eighteenth century double fortifications in the shape of a six-point star were constructed. To enter Almeida, the visitor must drive through three arched gateways.

Pousada de São Lourenço
6260 MANTEIGAS

B govt. rating
13 rooms
Phone (Covilhã) 47150
Telex 53992

DIRECTIONS: 50 km southwest of Guarda. If leaving Guarda, take N-18 south 25 km, then go northwest on 232 for 25 km to Manteigas. Approaching the ancient village of Manteigas, you will see the red-roofed pousada on a rise 12 twisting kilometers above and beyond the town.

Perched on a slope of Portugal's highest mountain range, Serra da Estrêla, the pousada is at an elevation of 5000 feet. Guest rooms are small but the lounge and dining room are roomy and both have fireplaces. Several couches are grouped around the lounge hearth, where a blazing fire is welcome on crisp fall nights. Guests gather there to watch television over an apéritif or simply to enjoy the warm glow in an amiable atmosphere.

Choices of hearty entrees in the pousada dining room could be *bacalhau assado* (baked cod), *peixe espada à la plancha* (grilled swordfish), or *cabrito assado* (roast lamb). Top off a meal with the delectable local Serra cheese and Zimbro brandy, a regional specialty.

On each corner of the central, open-sided dining room fireplace is a brass *candeia*, an oil-burning candelabrum with suspended pail to hold burnt matches, a pointed blade to adjust wicks and pincers to remove them, a shield to cut down glare, and a snuffer to extinguish flames from four apertures. The desire to purchase a *candeia* can lead to determined quests in town after town, but perseverance will pay off.

The town of Manteigas has been in existence since before Roman times.

ENVIRONS. Modern highrises dwarf the old section and castle of Guarda, the highest and coldest city in Portugal, at an altitude of 3412 feet. The advantage of its lofty location in the foothills of the Serra da Estrêla was realized by Romans, Visigoths, and Moors. Sancho I enlarged and fortified the town. His statue stands in the Praça Luis de Camões before the Manueline Gothic cathedral founded in the late fourteenth century and completed in 1540. Interesting homes from the 1500s to 1700s adorned with family crests edge the *praça*.

Mountainsides of the Zêzere River valley southeast of Manteigas are terraced with grapes.

Pousada de Santa Barbara

POVOA DAS QUARTAS,
3400 OLIVEIRA DO HOSPITAL

B govt. rating
16 rooms
Phone (Seia) 52252
Telex 53794

DIRECTIONS: 60 km southwest of Pousada de São Lourenço (Manteigas), 57 km south of Viseu. If coming via Highway N-232 from the east, turn south at its junction with Highway N-17 and head toward Oliveira do Hospital. *Póvoa* means small town, and Póvoa das Quartas is so little it isn't on most maps. Just past the sign announcing the *póvoa*, look for the Pousada sign and turn into the woods.

Overlooking the Alva River valley, whose cultivated hillsides are dotted with red-roofed houses, Pousada de Santa Barbara rests among aromatic pines. Built in the early 1970s, the pousada offers gracious accommodations. The split-level lounge is furnished colorfully and comfortably. Guest rooms, though small, hold all the requirements for a restful stay.

Gleaming tile floors lead to the dining room, where each table is decorated with fresh flowers. The menu offers a variety of entrees from *ensopado de cabrito* (lamb stew with vegetables) and *garoupa grelhada* (grilled grouper) to *galinha à Luzia* (roast chicken). As a first course choose from *caldo verde* (cabbage soup), *creme de aves* (cream of chicken), or *sopa de legumes* (vegetable soup). Regional wines are Dão *tintos*.

ENVIRONS. Nature went wild on the road between Póvoa das Quartas and Manteigas, having tossed giant boulders helter skelter. Minute vegetation clings to their forbidding surfaces. A marker west of Manteigas points out Cabeça do Velho—the old man's head is easily discernible in the rocky formations.

Oliveira do Hospital has a lovely setting amid olive trees, pines, and vineyards. Some of the town buildings are said to contain stones from the Roman era. In the village of Bobadela, 3 km west, there is a Roman arch. The twelfth-century Order of Hospitallers of Saint John of Jerusalem (now the Knights Templar of Malta) controlled the area, hence the "do Hospital" in the town's name.

If approaching the pousada from the north, consider stopping in the city of Viseu. Walls on three sides of the Praça da República are tiled with *azulejos* depicting nineteenth-century life. Viseu is a thriving center of agriculture and handcrafts such as lace, carpets, and black pottery.

Pousada de Santa Maria

7330 MARVAO

C govt. rating
9 rooms
Phone (Portalegre) 93201
Telex 42360

DIRECTIONS: 171 km southeast of Manteigas, 24 km north of Portalegre. Near the border with Spain. Reaching the pousada by car is a challenge. Marvão's medieval streets are wide enough for only one car. Look for a black wrought-iron circular sign reading Pousada de Santa Maria, extending over the street. Just beyond is a small parking space. If that is taken, drive a little farther and park on a tiny *praça*. You must ring for admittance to the pousada.

Marvão is a classic fortified village resting atop a severe rocky escarpment. The pousada was converted from a seventeenth-century mansion in the late 1940s. Guest rooms have high ceilings and are furnished with period pieces from the early 1900s. Two lounges, one with an *azulejo*-trimmed fireplace, easily accommodate overnight visitors and neighborhood drop-ins. The bar and dining room, added to the original building, have a 180-degree view east to distant mountains of Spain, north to the Serra da Estrêla, west to the Serra do São Mamede. With such a vista, an apéritif, lunch, or dinner is rendered unforgettable.

Dinner is served at 8 P.M. Suggested entrees include *linguado à marisqueira* (sole stuffed with shellfish), *tranches de goraz com almeijoas* (slices of fish with clams), and *perna de porco assada* (roast leg of pork). Two tasty soups are *gaspacho* and *açorda à alentejana* with a bread crumb base. Don't miss the pousada's dessert specialty, *sanhos* (SAHN-yoos), deep-fried fritters topped with nutmeg sauce.

TOURING MARVAO. A climb to the top of the ancient fortified castle is a must. Pass through four successive gates before reaching steps to the top of the ramparts. A village pamphlet says it was built by the Romans in 44 B.C. In 770 A.D., Moors captured the fortress and held it until its reconquest in 1116. Sancho II enlarged it and repaired the walls in 1226. Later, King Dinis, like his predecessors, appreciated its strategic value and strengthened the battlements, for Marvão commanded the countryside for miles even to the borders with Spain.

The castle withstood sieges during the War of Restoration in the 1640s and successfully resisted French troops in 1808, but was forced to yield to Dom Pedro's army in 1833 during the War of the Two Brothers.

The proud old houses of Marvão bear coats of arms and have Manueline windows and balconies festive with cascading flowers. Villagers say that large stones in the middle of streets were laid by the Romans.

ENVIRONS. Castelo de Vide, 14 km away, participated in the same battles as Marvão. The "new" part of town has a large *praça* featuring a statue of Pedro V, who visited in 1861, inviting, tree-shaded parks, white-washed houses,

Roman bridge at Portagem near Marvão

iron street signs, and a preserved medieval Judiaria, the Jewish quarter, where some homes are ornamented with Manueline doors and windows. Within the walled castle is the "old" part of town, a picturesque minivillage.

There are two other nearby sights to see. The exterior walls of the train station in Beira, 10 km to the north, hold a series of marvelous *azulejos* by Jorge Colaço. It is fun to see how many of the depicted famous landmarks of Portugal you can identify. Just follow signs through town to the Estação.

At Portagem, 5 km from Marvão, a Roman bridge still affords foot transport over a branch of the Sevéi River. It is particularly lovely in autumn with colorful foliage of graceful trees lining the banks.

The route between Manteigas (Parador de São Lourenço) and Marvão mostly along Highway N-18 is rich in many memorable scenes and is recommended highly. The road from Manteigas to Covilhã is the highest in Portugal and is sometimes closed until the end of April. This is the recreational area known as Penhas da Saúde, receiving the country's only measurable snowfall. In autumn there is little traffic through mountains that are bleak save for scanty plant life watered by trickling springs. Nave de Santo António is a winter sports settlement with a lift more than half a mile long carrying skiers high above a broad valley floor.

Covilhã is a busy town known for its *queijo da Serra,* tangy cheese made from ewes' milk, and for its woolen industry that supplies two-thirds of the country's yarn. On the route through town is a church whose exterior is covered completely with brilliant blue *azulejos.*

The 18-km stretch from Covilhã to Fundão, also a woolen center, takes travelers through pine forests where occasional roadside stands sell flowers, apples, pears, and figs. Olive, fruit, and some orange trees then give way to large fields of cereal grains. There are few houses to be seen for many miles.

The outline of Castelo Branco's remaining fortifications frame today's busy industrial city. One of Portugal's finest gardens surrounds the seventeenth-century Bishop's Palace. Walk down a stone staircase bordered on one side by statues of former kings and on the other by Apostles and saints. Take time for a stroll past reflecting pools, clipped hedges, and flower beds before entering the regional museum. On display are archeological finds, paintings, tapestries, antique furniture and a display of embroidered bedspreads, *colchas,* a famous textile product of Castelo Branco. *Colchas* are for sale in many of the city's shops.

South of Castelo Branco, encampments of Gypsies give a different dimension to the ever-changing scene: smoke curling from smoldering fires, low-sagging tents, crude wagons and carts, handsome well-tended horses, and naked, gamboling children.

Pousada de Santa Luzia

7350 ELVAS

B govt. rating
11 rooms
Phone 62194
Telex 12469

DIRECTIONS: 73 km southeast of Marvão, 17 km west of Badajoz, Spain, 91 km northeast of Evora. To reach the pousada, don't enter *cidade centro*. Follow signs to Espanha (Spain). Those approaching from Badajoz will see the pousada to the left of a signal light.

The kitchen of this pousada has a well-deserved reputation for excellence throughout the Iberian Peninsula. A commodious bar-lounge and inside and outside dining areas lure local customers, busloads from Spain, and overnight guests of the pousada. If you have not done so, here is the place to try *bacalhau*, cod. *Bacalhau dourado* is fried in egg and served with french fries. Other delectables include *lulas recheadas* (stuffed squid), *pargo assado à portuguesa* (roast sea bream), *arroz de pato à pousada* (oven-baked duckling served on rice), *favas guisadas à caseira* (broad bean stew), and the popular *carne de porco à alentejana* (pork with clams).

Start lunch or dinner with *acepipes variados*, assorted hors d'oeuvres. Save room for a choice of two *sobremesas*. *Gelado de natas com chocolate* is vanilla ice cream frozen in molds, sliced, and covered with a rich high-calorie chocolate sauce. *Cerieaia com ameixas de Elvas* is a sponge cake covered with a delicious sauce of famous Elvas plums. Boxes of dried plums, Elvas's well-known confection, are for sale at the pousada desk. House wines are *tintos* from Borba and Redondo. The wine list is extensive, as are a la carte menu choices.

TOURING ELVAS. The vulnerability of Elvas, so close to Spain, demanded early and continued fortification. The road into the city from the north passes eighteenth-century Forte de Nossa Senhora da Graça. Two fortified walls built in the thirteenth century and a third added in the seventeenth and eighteenth centuries enclosed the old city, whose castle, built on Roman foundations by the Moors, was regained by the Portuguese in 1226. Outside the ramparts, visible from the pousada, is seventeenth-century Santa Luzia Fortress, protecting the city on the east. For an appreciation of the stronghold, drive around its perimeter, a distance of five kilometers.

Elvas's most striking monument is the still operational Amoreira Aqueduct, constructed betwen 1498 and 1622. Its length of five kilometers, height of 34 feet, and 800 arches make it the largest aqueduct in the country.

The journey between Marvão and Elvas is a pastoral delight. The good road goes through Portalegre, Arronches, and Santa Eulália. Portalegre's seventeenth-century mansions resulted from a period in the city's life when silk industries brought prosperity to upper middle-class merchants.

The Alentejo lies south of Portalegre. In this vast plains area of southern Portugal, cork and olive trees share large land holdings planted in cereal grains. Santa Eulália is a charming community of whitewashed houses with typical Alentejo chimneys. Either square or cylindrical, they have open-work designs and are topped with a decorative finial. Flowers and glossy-leaved citrus trees border broad sidewalks.

Pousada
da Rainha Santa Isabel

7100 ESTREMOZ

CH govt. rating
23 rooms
Phone 22618
Telex 43885

DIRECTIONS: 42 km west of Elvas. Ramparts and keep of the thirteenth-century castle built by King Dinis are seen on the approach
to Estremoz. Driving through town, stay right up the hill. When
you see the drawbridge, turn and go through the gate.

Pousada da Rainha Santa Isabel, acclaimed one of Portugal's finest, is within castle walls and adjacent to the keep
that was home to Isabel of Aragón, wife of King Dinis.
Parts of the old castle have been incorporated into the
pousada structure. Vaulted ceilings 22 feet high loom over
the salon-reception hall. Tiled floors banded with broad
blocks of polished marble lead to a grand ballroom-sized
lounge where arched windows are set in walls seven feet
thick. A painting of the wistful, saintly queen looks down
on twentieth-century bar transactions. Corridors, solar-
iums, and guest rooms hold such priceless furniture and
artifacts as carved chests, gilt mirrors, and canopied beds.
Marble from nearby quarries has been the prime material
for floors, stairways, walls, and tables.

In the regal dining room, gourmet food is served under
the direction of a charming young maitre d'. The menu
offers *gaspacho à alentejana* (in this version, vegetables are

not pureed but finely chopped and seasoned with pork sausage), *ensopado de cação* (a stew of white fish in wine sauce flavored with coriander, served with boiled potatoes and crisp chunks of bread), and *ensopado de borrego* (a lamb stew with white wine sauce, typical of this region). Order *borrego assado* and you will receive succulent roast lamb with fresh cauliflower, tiny new potatoes, and half a baked tomato. Here salad dressing is more than the typical Iberian oil and vinegar, for it contains sour cream, mayonnaise, and spices in addition to oil and vinegar. The rye bread served with entrees is another welcome departure. The most typical *sobremesa* is *sopa dourada* ("golden soup"). It is a pudding made of egg yolks, cinnamon, and croutons, topped with crushed almonds. Another dessert favorite in this area is *queijadas de Evora,* a delicious cheesecake. Regional wines are from Borba and Redondo, full-bodied reds. It was at Estremoz that we discovered one of the finest wines in Portugal, Frangoneiro. Relatively expensive, the *branco* and *tinto* are rather rare as the winery is quite small.

Ask at the pousada desk how to see the chapel of the castle. Entrance to the *capela* is through decorative iron gates and up a staircase. Three large scenes in *azulejos* depict legends of Isabel. But alas, the Miracle of the Roses is not one of them. It is such a lovely story that it must be told anyway.

Isabel used to rob the castle kitchens to feed the poor of the neighborhood. She hid tasty morsels in her apron. Eventually King Dinis learned of her handouts and accosted her one day as she was about to make her rounds. He demanded she open her apron and when she did, down drifted rose petals. The legend continues that when she stooped to gather the petals, they turned into gold coins, which she soon distributed to the needy.

A painting above the sets of *azulejos* shows Isabel with an armful of roses. The same is true of the sixteenth-century wooden carving of the queen above the altar.

In the first group of *azulejos* King Dinis is having an angry confrontation with the king of Castilla as Isabel steps in to separate them. The second recounts the time when a city was threatened with flooding and Isabel parted the swirling waters. In the third, the castle of Leiria looms in the background as Isabel rescues a drowning child.

Like in Coimbra, a leper and Saint Francis flank Queen Saint Isabel over the altar. Ask to see a tiny room above and behind the altar. Here, one is told, the saintly queen slept on nights when she could escape the importunities of Dinis, who sired seven illegitimate offspring.

There is much to see in the vicinity of this pousada. Saturday is market day in Estremoz. Held in the main square, the market features an extensive display of Estremoz pottery, from jugs and bowls to naive figurines.

SIDE TRIPS FROM ESTREMOZ. Plan on about three hours for a visit to Vila Viçosa and the marble quarries near Borba. Vila Viçosa was once the domain of the dukes of Bragança after the second duke, Dom Fernando, elected to build his residence there. The third duke, also Fernando, was executed in Evora by João II for plots against the monarchy. In 1501, tired of the drafty old palace, Jaime, the fourth duke, began construction of the present *paço*. It remained for successive dukes to put finishing touches on the palace where marriages between princes and princesses and extravagant *festas* for aristocracy took place. Courtly activity then shifted from Vila Viçosa to Lisboa when the eighth duke of Bragança ascended the throne as João IV.

A bronze equestrian statue of João, who started the Bragança dynasty, stands in majesty before the palace. The entrance hall where one waits for the guided tour to begin is lined with paintings of Portugal's kings from Afonso through Manoel.

The Braganças loved to hunt and at Vila Viçosa they had 5000 acres in which to pursue their sport. They must have been wealthy ecologists at heart because not much of a deer's anatomy was wasted. A huge kitchen spit beneath a 60-foot chimney turned many a juicy venison carcass. Six thousand copper pots simmered savory condiments. The ornamentation of tables, chairs, and chandeliers was fashioned from countless antlers.

The ducal palace is furnished as it was during the days of King Carlos, Queen Amélia, and their children. One feels their presence and wishes the poor king had been a commoner so as to have developed his remarkable talent to the fullest. His charcoal drawings, landscapes, and portraits hang in many rooms of the palace. Perhaps his unquestionable ability came from his grandfather, Fernando II, whose artwork is also on display.

After a tour of the *paço*, which takes about an hour, go toward the castle and pause for a look at a church faced with *azulejos*. Behind and to one side of the church is a cemetery where family mausoleums have lace-curtained windows revealing pictures of the deceased. Seldom does one see a cemetery in Portugal not bedecked with flowers by townspeople.

A drawbridge over an empty moat leads to the thirteenth-century castle built by King Dinis. Generations later, the ramparts were strengthened by walls still encircling the old town. Be sure to see the Porto dos Nós (gate of knots) north of the palace square. The Manueline portal, trimmed with stone seamen's knots, is the last vestige of sixteenth-century walls that once surrounded the palace. Today, teenagers stream through the gate on their way to school.

From Vila Viçosa to Borba there is one marble quarry after another. Marble, by the way, is Portugal's number two export after cork. Do take time to investigate the fascinating pits, which yield marble for domestic and foreign markets. Curbs, sidewalks, doorways, and windowsills of Borba's homes are marble. Buy a bottle of Borba *vinho* and you will obtain a prize label to add to your collection.

At Evora Monte, 11 km southwest of Estremoz, is a rather unusual castle. Recently restored and electrified, it has three floors and walls about ten feet thick. From the top is a panoramic view of Estremoz and a countryside dotted with olive trees and tiny white villages. Plaques state that the castle dates from the twelfth century. It was reconstructed by Dinis in 1306 and again by Don Juan in 1532. It was here that victorious Pedro forced brother Miguel to abdicate the throne in favor of his niece, Maria. Thus the War of the Two Brothers came to an end and Miguel was sent into exile.

Pousada dos Lóios

7000 EVORA

CH govt. rating
32 rooms
Phone 24051
Telex 43288

DIRECTIONS: 45 km southwest of Estremoz.

Pousada dos Lóios was converted in 1965 from conventual buildings and the chapter house of fifteenth-century Convento dos Lóios. Floors of the reception hall are patterned in black, rust, and white marble. A balustrade of pink marble completes the magnificent staircase on whose wall hangs a splendid new Arraiolos carpet.

Guest rooms lead off an upstairs gallery of glass-enclosed arches. The eagle emblem of the Lóios monks appears on headboards of the beds. Arraiolos rugs lie between twin beds. Ten cells of the monastery have been transformed into rooms and although low doorways seem to presage a cramped interior, ceilings are of normal height and windows provide a welcome view of an orange grove. Former cloisters enclosing an open courtyard planted in orange trees have been shielded with glass and serve as a rambling dining hall. (In late autumn and winter, a smaller enclosed dining room is used because of heating problems.) The combination of Mudejar and Manueline architecture lends an elegant atmosphere to dining.

Featured on the pousada menu are *filetes de pescada com arroz de legumes* (slices of white fish with vegetables and rice), *perna de borrego assada à padeiro* (roast leg of lamb with potatoes and onions), *frango na púcara* (stewed chicken), *omeleta de frango* (chicken omelette), *febras de porco grelhadas* (grilled pork steaks), and *espetada de frango* (breast of chicken on a spit).

TOURING EVORA. Rodrigo Afonso de Melo, a courageous captain who had survived the Battle of Tangier and who had served as advisor to Afonso V, received permission from João II to build a religious institution on a site that had once held the old castle of Evora. Rodrigo wanted not only a religious house but a proper mausoleum for his family. The first stone of Convento dos Lóios, dedicated to Saint John the Evangelist, was laid in 1485. Rodrigo died before its completion in 1491. If the church joined to the pousada is closed, inquire at the desk and the keeper of the keys will be summoned.

The interior of the sanctuary, except floor and ceiling, is covered with *azulejos* portraying the life of Saint Laurence Justinian, founder of the Order of Saint John. In a small cubicle off the sacristy is a portion of Roman wall discovered when the church was undergoing restoration in 1958. Beneath the floor of the church are the original monastery cistern, a communal grave of hundreds of monks, and tombs of Rodrigo and his family.

Although Evora's past eminence has waned, enough remains to warrant its reputation as the Museum of Portugal. Its origin is remote, but that it was inhabited by Germanic tribes is certain because the effort to conquer it was recorded by Pliny and Strabo. Sertorius fortified Ebora, as it was called under Caesar. A Roman temple believed to have been dedicated to Diana was built on the highest point of an acropolis during the reigns of Trajan and Hadrian. The temple was destroyed in the fifth century, and some of its remnants were used to fortify the town's castle during the Middle Ages. Other ruins of the temple later served as a slaughterhouse. In 1871 reconstruction returned the monument to a semblance of its original glory. The handsome relic, with capitals and bases of Estremoz marble, stands across from the pousada.

The Moors took possession of "Iabura" in the early eighth century and remained until driven out by forces of Afonso Henriques led by the outlaw warrior Gerald the Fearless in 1165. Moorish architecture and the jumbled layout of the town remain from that period. Narrow cobbled streets, some joined by arches, are edged with white houses that have flower boxes on second-story grilled windows. Purchase a guidebook at the pousada desk and take a walking tour of Evora, whose buildings date from the fifteenth and sixteenth centuries.

Many kings lived from time to time in Evora. Their august presences demanded artisans' products of gold, silver, wood carving, and tapestries. During the sixteenth century, the existence of so many outstanding artists established Evora as a cultural center. Cardinal Henrique, first archbishop of the city and later king of Portugal,

Casa dos Ossos in the Church of São Francisco, Evora.

founded the university in 1551 and endowed many fine buildings. King Sebastião lived in the palace of the dukes of Cadaval while studying at the university, which was run by Jesuits. In 1759 Pombal ordered them out of the country and the university was closed. It was reopened in 1841 as a national high school and today is a state university.

Facing the Temple of Diana and adjacent to the pousada is the Regional Museum. Roman artifacts found in Arraiolos, Beja, and Evora, paintings from the Middle Ages through the Renaissance, and sculptures old and new are on display in the sixteenth-century bishop's palace. Embellished Manueline portals lead from room to room. Arraiolos rugs are for sale in a gift shop of the museum.

There are two very unusual places to see. In the Church of São Francisco is gruesome Casa dos Ossos. The inscription over its entrance has this chilling message: "We bones that are here await your bones." The story goes that a sixteenth-century monk decided once and for all to press home the value of meditation by retrieving bones of over 5000 deceased padres. These were used to cover every inch of the walls and pillars. As an added reminder, a complete skeleton hangs in one corner.

The other extraordinary sight is the Hermitage of São Brás. You may be too weary to locate it on foot, but watch for it as you are leaving Evora. Turrets, spires, towers, and arches of the curious building were once incorporated into the city's defense system. Later, during the Inquisition, tragic autos-da-fé were conducted on the grounds.

SIDE TRIPS FROM EVORA. Avis, 63 km north of Evora, looks more attractive from a distance but the drive is pleasant. Gypsy camps are numerous in this sector of the Alentejo. Extensive grain fields, clumps of olive trees, and gentle hillocks dotted with grazing sheep form a harmonious landscape. On autumn weekends, parties of hunters and their hounds and families relaxing over picnic lunches are seen along the roadside.

It was in Avis that Afonso Henriques established the oldest religious-military order in Europe to fight the Moors. Its name was changed periodically until King Dinis made it a purely national order free from domination by Rome and gave it the title Order of Christ. João I was a former master of the order, as was his son Prince Henry the Navigator, who used its wealth to finance many of the early voyages of discovery.

If you have several hours to spare, drive to Arraiolos for a *tapête*. Arraiolos carpets hang on walls of palaces, castles, and over stairs and corridors of many pousadas. These rugs, practically works of art, are done in cross-stitch by hand using brilliantly colored wool. Orders are received from all over the world and if you are lucky, you will find one available to purchase. Should the size or design be not exactly to your liking, a carpet of your choice can be made up and shipped home. One that is six and a half by three and a half feet folds into a neat bundle to be squeezed into your luggage. Such a rug costs about $130 and makes a worthy memento of a trip to Portugal. Ask to be shown the workroom to observe fingers flying steadily, stopping briefly for the weaver to glance at a pattern. Shops close from noon to 3 P.M.

Pousada de São Gens
7830 SERPA

B govt. rating
17 rooms
Phone (Beja) 90327
Telex 43651

DIRECTIONS: 100 km southeast of Evora. Appearing as the crown of a hill of olive trees, the pousada is located 3 km south of Serpa off the road to Spain.

Cool tile-floored guest rooms open onto balconies equipped with lounge chairs. Slopes of the pousada grounds planted in young silvery-leaved olive trees lead to a sea of newly plowed farmland, property of a white, red-tiled, multi-chimneyed *casa da quinta* (farmhouse). Bleating cries of lambs, far-off voices of children, low drones of tractors, and merry chirping of birds waft through warm, dry autumn air. The pousada is the perfect place for lazy contemplation and relaxation.

Dishes typical of the Alentejo are served in the pleasant dining room. Select from *cação com molho de alho* (dogfish with garlic sauce), *migas à Serpa* (pork fried with coarse bread crumbs), and *ensopado de borrego* (lamb stew). For after dinner, enjoy famous Serpa cheese. House wines are those from the nearby Vidigueira cooperative.

The town of Serpa, though retaining old castle ruins and a medieval gate, is now an agricultural center. It was an important Roman outpost and was conquered from the Moors by Gerald the Fearless in 1166.

SIDE TRIPS FROM SERPA. After a stroll through town, drive 29 km northeast to Moura, also called Vila da Moura, village of the Moorish maid. A tragic legend tells that on the morning of her wedding, Salúquia, daughter of a Moorish leader, watched from castle heights for the arrival of her husband-to-be. Her vigil was hopeless because her lover, lord of a nearby castle, and his retinue had been slain by Christian warriors, who then donned the garments of their victims and entered the castle. When Salúquia discovered their treachery, she leaped to her death.

Moura was held by the Moslems until 1233 and has an Arab atmosphere. A solid row of low white dwellings rings the castle perimeter. Saint John the Baptist Church has a handsome Manueline door emblazoned with armillary spheres. Go beyond the church to a shady garden. There in the midst of a fountained pool, Salúquia's castle in miniature perpetuates the legend of Moura.

The road southwest of Evora, Highway N-18, presents an interesting picture of the Alentejo. Wheat fields extend for miles, while higher elevations are reserved for cork and olive trees. Cattle and sheep graze endlessly on patches of stubble. Foundations, doors, and windows of village houses are banded with bright blue. Portel's thirteenth-century castle ruins are seen to the east. Gypsy wagons heaped with family belongings crawl toward a conclave near Vidigueira.

Beja, 29 km west of the pousada, is dominated by massive grain elevators, not its thirteenth-century castle built by King Dinis. A Roman colony—Pax Julia—founded in 48 B.C. by Julius Caesar, it was developed into the marketing center of the Alentejo and today remains capital of the rich wheat belt. An archway, parts of city walls, and an aqueduct remain from days of Roman rule.

Wonderful views of the countryside are seen from the top of Torre de Menagem, the castle keep restored in 1940: on the northwest, the Serra de Sintra, on the north Evora, and to the east the Spanish mountains.

Beja achieved fame in the literary world when the "Portuguese letters" appeared in France in 1669. Five love letters were said to have been written by a nun in the Conceição Convent to Count de Chamilly, who had fought on the Alentejo against Castilians. The count was evidently not steadfast, as Sister Mariana Alcoforado's letters were full of reproach for his faithlessness. Today a regional museum is housed in the convent. There is a reconstructed cell window through which Mariana and the count may have conversed.

Pousada de São Brás

8150 SAO BRAS DE ALPORTEL

B govt. rating
15 rooms
Phone (Faro) 42305
Telex 56945

DIRECTIONS: 18 km north of Faro, 44 km west of Ayamonte, Spain. The pousada sits on a hill 3 km north of São Brás off the road to Lisboa.

The pousada is gleaming white, roofed with red tile, and has typical Alentejo chimneys, one cylindrical and another square. Guest room balconies look out over the town. On clear days the Atlantic shimmers on the horizon. A cozy lounge is made even more inviting on cool nights by the warmth of logs blazing in a stone fireplace. Crunchy nuts are served with apéritifs.

Over the fireplace in the circular dining room hangs a *molim*, a brightly decorated horse collar often seen in the Algarve. Food is excellent and the choices are extensive. Some suggested entrees are *coquinhos grelhados com molho de manteiga* (grilled cuttlefish with butter sauce), *caldeirada de borrega à pousada* (stewed lamb), *frango frito com molho tomate* (fried chicken with tomato sauce), *bifinhos de vitela com cogumelos* (veal steaks with mushrooms), and *filetes de peixe estufados com molho de camarão* (fried fish slices with shrimp sauce). The dessert cart is loaded with such items as apple tart, jelly roll, and *tarta de laranja*, a delicate orange sponge cake. House wines are red and whites from the cooperative in Lagoa.

SIDE TRIPS FROM SAO BRAS DE ALPORTEL. Pousada de São Brás is so charming and comfortable that a stay of two or more days is called for in order to explore the eastern part of the Algarve. Vila Real de São António, across from Ayamonte in Spain, was the creation of the marquis of Pombal. He commanded a town to be built to counter Ayamonte's advantageous position; within five months there was a city with houses like Lisboa's and black and white mosaic pavements.

Ferries to Ayamonte run every half hour beginning at 8 A.M. During fall and winter only one ferry is in operation and the whole process takes about an hour and a half.

Between Vila Real and Tavira is a series of truck farms where orange trees share soil with lettuce and other green vegetables. Typical Algarve tile-faced *casas* with their distinctive chimneys are beautified by riotous hibiscus, poinsettias, bougainvillea, and pyracantha. Then, closer to Tavira, along with the ubiquitous grape and olive, almond trees appear. The introduction of the almond to the Algarve is explained by a Portuguese folktale.

There was once a Moorish ruler in the area whose bride, a Scandinavian princess, yearned for the pristine snow of her homeland. The sympathetic bridegroom ordered the planting of hundreds of almond trees. One winter morning, the princess was overwhelmed with joy when she looked out to a never-ending whiteness of flowering almond trees.

The spongy swamps surrounding Faro, 18 km south of

São Brás, are easily seen from a distance, looking surprisingly like their rendition on a map. Faro was destroyed in the 1755 earthquake and the rebuilt town is charming. Visit the cathedral, which was reconstructed in the eighteenth century and which contains fine seventeenth-century *azulejos*, the Maritime Museum displaying models of fishing vessels used in Algarve waters, and the old town to the south of the city's garden and park. Then return to the small boat harbor. In a quayside restaurant, enjoy lunch while watching intriguing water activity.

In Vilamoura, 25 km northwest of Faro and 5 km south of Highway N-125, Portugal's finest anchorage is stocked with yachts from all over Europe as well as local craft. Most vessels fly the British flag, but the Stars and Stripes waves from a few. Modern apartments within the marina are for sale or rent. The whole surrounding area is burgeoning with vacation villas and apartment complexes.

A short jaunt northwest of Pousada de São Brás offers nature's rare color scheme of orange-trunked cork trees growing on hillsides cloaked in delicate, rosy heather. After cork trees are stripped of their bark the trunks are coated with an orange solution. Trees may be divested of their bark every eight to ten years. Stacks of cork awaiting shipment are often seen along the road.

Cork, one of Portugal's most valuable exports, awaits shipment.

Pousada do Infante
8650 SAGRES

CH govt. rating
21 rooms
Phone (Portimão) 64222
Telex 57491

DIRECTIONS: 124 km west of São Brás, across the bay from Cabo São Vicente, Portugal's southwesternmost tip.

Pousada do Infante, named for Prince Henry the Navigator, is one of Portugal's most popular pousadas and underwent rehabilitation in 1985. Guest room balconies look out beyond a grassy terrace to the sea, where there is always some sort of vessel on the horizon whether it be a fishing boat, coastal freighter, or a Portuguese naval craft. Blue-green waves spew foam onto sandy beaches.

On cool autumn and winter nights, guests gather before the fire in a dramatic circular lounge extending on one end to the bar and on the other to a dining room that has tile wainscoting with alternating images of armillary spheres and crosses of the Order of Christ.

Choices in the dining room are varied and well prepared: *parguinho grelhado com molho de manteiga* (grilled bream with butter sauce), *tranchas douradas de peixe com maionese* (sliced fish with mayonnaise, rice, and salad), *ganso de vitela estufado* (veal stew), and *figado de vitela na grelha* (grilled calves' liver). As a starter, *sopa do mar,* seafood soup, sets the stage. *Pudim de claras com caramelo* is a light, satisfying custard with a caramel sauce. The extensive wine list includes all of the excellent wines of Portugal.

SIDE TRIPS FROM SAGRES. A stay of two days to see nearby sights is recommended. A short distance away is the Fortaleza, site of Prince Henry's school of navigation. Spurred by messianic zeal, political and monetary ambitions, and a thirst for more knowledge of the west coast of Africa and the world beyond Europe, Henry (Henrique) established his school and observatory at Sagres. Aided by scholars and cartographers, he planned expeditions and perfected navigational instruments. Although he himself never participated in exploratory voyages, his captains changed the way Europeans perceived the world by traveling to the Madeiras, Azores, and Cape Verde Islands, and by eventually rounding the Cape of Good Hope and reaching India and Asia. Within 50 years of Henry's death, Portuguese reached the interior of Africa and claimed sovereignty over Brazil.

Before walking or driving around the promontory, be sure to see a film (in English) about the life of Prince Henry shown daily at 3:30 in a small auditorium several hundred feet in back of the Turismo office.

Graça Chapel, with the cape in the background, is where Prince Henry is believed to have worshiped. Notice a large compass rose laid out in stones, presumed to date from Henry's time—it only appeared in 1928, when parts of the fort were being reconstructed. The sundial is the original used by marine scholars.

Cabo São Vicente, the westernmost tip of Europe, was known to medieval sailors as "o fim do mundo," the end of the world. Its traditional name derives from the time when the remains of Saint Vincent, who was slain in Valencia, were brought to the cape by monks in the eighth century. When Afonso Henriques ordered the relics sent to Lisboa, it is said that two ravens, one fore and one aft the ship, never left the vessel and were observed on its entrance into Lisboa's harbor. The ship and ravens form the crest of Portugal's capital city.

Monks installed a lighthouse on the cape hundreds of years ago and maintained it until government takeover in the 1920s. Today its light is the most powerful in Europe, casting a beam seen 60 miles out to sea.

Fig, almond, and olive groves are the predominant agricultural features around Lagos, 43 km east of Sagres. To harvest olives, workers first spread tarps under the trees and shake branches vigorously, then stoop to gather the fallen fruit.

It was in Lagos that Prince Henry constructed his caravels for the voyages of discovery. The main avenue parallels a channel where fishing boats are marooned at low tide. Broad sidewalks are tessellated in black and white. A statue of Henry commands a large square between the harbor and the old town. Next to ruins of the fortress that guarded the entrance to Lagos harbor is a statue of Gil Eanes commemorating the day in 1434 when he led an expedition to Cape Bojador on the west coast of Africa, just south of the Canary Islands. On a world map this doesn't look like much of a feat, but Eanes's was a great step forward as succeeding fleets sailed farther and farther until Vasco da Gama rounded the Cape of Good Hope in 1498. In addition to all these historic monuments, Lagos has many inviting small restaurants, pubs (so-called because many Britons live there), and shops.

At Lagoa, 26 km east of Lagos, head north for a short side trip to Silves. Citrus, peach, and fig trees alternate with eucalyptus forests and vineyards through a productive valley irrigated by Ribeira de Odeluca.

On banks of the Arade River, Silves was Xelb, the Moorish capital of the Algarve. Idrisi, an Arab historian of those days, recorded that it had a "fine appearance, with attractive buildings and well-furnished bazaars. Its inhabitants are Yemenite Arabs and others, who speak pure Arabic, compose poetry, and are eloquent in speech and elegant in manners, both the upper and the lower classes." All that remain today are remnants of old walls, a restored red sandstone castle, and a cathedral in the old part of town. In a park on grounds of the castle is a statue of Sancho I, who captured Silves from the Moors in 1189. The cistern of the castle still serves as the town's reservoir. From crenellated ramparts are wonderful views of peach and almond orchards in the valley of the Arade River. In the cathedral below the castle-fortress are tombs said to be those of crusaders who happened by and aided Sancho in his victory.

Albufeira is a pleasant place to stop between Sagres and Faro. Once an Arab stronghold, it is now a fishing town and seaside resort with marvelous shops. Follow narrow cobbled streets downhill to a large square, the gathering

place for natives and tourists, which is bordered with outdoor restaurants and shops selling souvenirs and fine gifts.

Pousada de Santa Clara
7665 SANTA CLARA-A-VELHA

B govt. rating
6 rooms
Phone (Odemira) 52250
Telex 56231

DIRECTIONS: 111 km northeast of Sagres.

Pousada de Santa Clara overlooks a *barragem* (dam) constructed for irrigation purposes. Concrete channels seen
from guest rooms follow the contour of the hills. You must
park below and walk upstairs to the pousada entrance
where the reception desk also serves as bar.

The food is tasty, hearty fare appropriate for engineers
and employees working at the dam as well as overnight
visitors. Specialties include *trutas à moleira* (fresh trout), *perna
de porco assada com molho de maçã* (roast pork with applesauce), *peixe espada grelhado* (grilled swordfish), *medalhões de
vitela à rosmaninho* (medallions of veal flavored with rose-
mary). As an appetizer, choose either *creme de alho francês*
(cream of leek soup) or *sopa de cação à alentejana* (dogfish
soup—dogfish is a small shark).

From the pousada extend hiking paths almost completely roofed by graceful mimosa trees full of singing birds.
You may be lucky enough to meet fellow guests willing to
share their profound knowledge of the flora and fauna lining the paths.

ENVIRONS. Highway N-266 south of the pousada goes
through the Serra de Monchique, whose rocky, terraced
slopes support cork and pine forests. Caldas de Monchique was once an important health spa where medicinal
springs, known even to the Romans, brought relief to those
with rheumatism. In 1495, João II came to Caldas to drink
the waters in an unsuccessful attempt to cure dropsy, for
he died soon after his arrival.

Pousada de São Tiago
7540 SANTIAGO DO CACEM

B govt. rating
7 rooms
Phone 22459
Telex 16166

DIRECTIONS: 78 km west of Beja, 87 km northwest of Santa Clara-a-Velha. The pousada is on the northern outskirts of town on the road to Lisboa. At the pousada sign, enter a wooded glen and park in front of an ivy-covered structure that must have been the coach house of the old mansion turned pousada. Walk upstairs to a dark green door and ring for admittance.

From windows of the high-ceilinged guest rooms upstairs, the white, red-roofed houses of Santiago can be seen extending to the castle, said to have been built by the Knights Templar. The ramparts, all that remain, enclose the town cemetery, whose evergreens seem to sprout from the bulwarks.

The dining room fireplace, flanked and fronted by couches, is the focal point for afternoon cocktails. A perfect fire is laid by first positioning twigs one by one into a pyramid that is ignited, then rolling onto the flames a charred log that has seen many a fire. Dinner is served at 8 P.M. by candlelight.

After *acepipes variados* (assorted hors d'oeuvres) or *açorda com coentros e ovos* (traditional Alentejo garlic soup with bread and a poached egg floating on top), consider the following entrees: *arroz de grelos com pasteis de bacalhau* (cod patties with vegetable rice), *frango com cerveja* (chicken simmered in beer), or another Alentejo favorite, *carne de porco com migas* (pork fried with bread crumbs). If you are stopping by for lunch, select a cheese omelette with salad.

ENVIRONS. Excavations of a Roman city are being carried out a few kilometers from Santiago at Mirobriga.

Until a few years ago, Sines, 17 km west of Santiago, was a recommended side trip. It was a charming village with an active fishing fleet. Now, it is the center of extensive oil refineries handling tankers of 500,000 tons.

The road south of Santiago do Cacém goes through miles of cork forests with occasional stretches of plowed fields and a few small houses. Farms are larger and farm houses more numerous to the north. Animal life includes white herons perched nonchalantly on the backs of munching ewes.

Pousada de Vale de Gaio

7580 ALCACER DO SAL

B govt. rating
6 rooms
Phone (Setúbal) 66100
Telex 15118

DIRECTIONS: 75 km northeast of Santiago do Cacém.

Pousada de Vale de Gaio was built as a lodge for hunters, who mainly net *coelhos* (rabbits). Guest rooms are small but adequately comfortable. Adjoining baths have individual water tanks mounted on the walls, similar to those found in England. Thus the guest is assured of instant hot water, a necessity sometimes lacking in pousadas having conventional boilers.

Guests as well as citizens of Alcácer enjoy good food in the restful, attractive dining room. Appetizers include *melão com presunto* (melon with ham similar to prosciutto), *gaspacho à alentejana*, or *sopa juliana* (vegetable soup). Choose one or two of these entrees: *costoletas de cabrito primaveril* (lamb chops), *bifes de atum salteados* (tuna steaks), *caldeirada à barragem* (fresh fish stew), or *figado de vitela à portuguesa* (grilled calves' liver).

Castle remains and parts of old city walls are still evident in Alcácer do Sal, which means palace of salt. In Roman days it was called Salacia, even then named for its salt production. To the Moors it was Qasr Abi Danis, a fortified town at the mouth of the Sado River. Afonso Henriques was wounded in an attempt to take the fortress. A second try was made a few years later but it, too, failed. The site was eventually captured in 1217 with the help of crusaders.

Alcácer is situated on the Sado River, surrounded by rice fields and salt marshes. For centuries it had been the main marketing center for Alentejo grain. But now, thanks to a system of canals supplied by the Sado, it is the center of rich rice paddies. Women can be seen bent over, tending the fields. They wear black "Homberg" hats over colorful scarves to protect their necks from the sun. This head gear is typical for working women along the Algarve.

Pousada de São Filipe
2900 SETUBAL

CH govt. rating
15 rooms
Phone 23844
Telex 44655

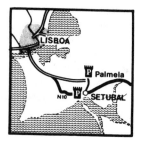

DIRECTIONS: 40 km southeast of Lisboa. Castelo de São Filipe is seen by those approaching Setúbal in either direction, on heights overlooking the harbor. Signs reading Castelo and Pousada appear along the main drag, Avenida Luiza Todi. At the second Pousada marker, motorists driving west should make an immediate right turn, then a left onto Rua de São Filipe. Proceed up the narrow street and drive through gates leading to the castle. There is no road through the ramparts so cars are parked outside the walls. It is rather a struggle with luggage, reaching the pousada entrance via underground stone steps.

Advance reservations are essential at Pousada de São Filipe because of its proximity to Lisboa. Request a waterfront room, for the view encompasses busy shipyards, fishing docks, pleasure craft marina, vessels plying the Bay of Sado, and Hovercraft breezing to Troia Peninsula. Amenities at the popular pousada include well-furnished rooms, several attractive lounges, a cozy *adega*, and a second-floor dining room where gourmet food is served by white-jacketed waiters at 7:45 P.M. Three fish specialties of the house are *sopa rica de peixe* (fish soup), *robalinhos à São Filipe* (small bass), and *salmonetes à setubalense* (red mullet). Meat entrees include *escalopes de vitela com Madeira* (veal cutlets in Madeira wine), *cabrito assado à ribatejana* (roast kid), and *leitão à Bairrada* (roast suckling pig). Be sure to order a Setúbal moscatel with dessert or fruit.

Castelo de São Filipe was built by the Spaniards in 1590. Philip II was concerned about belligerent citizens and he wanted to keep an eye on Troia Peninsula, suspecting the British of setting up military installations. In 1766, the castle-fortress became a prison and lost its historic and aesthetic value until conversion into a pousada in 1965. Plaques on walls of the underground staircase record visits of Maria II and husband Fernando and of João V and sons.

The tiny castle chapel is decorated with blue *azulejos* painted by Policarpo de Oliveira Bernardes in 1736. The tiles recount the life of São Filipe (Saint Philip—not Philip II of Spain).

SETUBAL AND ENVIRONS. Try to allow a full day for exploring Setúbal, according to legend founded by Túbal, son of Cain. Roman invaders called it Cetobriga. During Afonso Henriques's successful struggle to drive out the Moors, much of the city was destroyed. It remained for son Sancho I to rebuild the ancient port.

But Setúbal was leveled by the 1755 earthquake. For that reason, buildings and avenues are in the style promulgated by the marquis of Pombal. Just beyond the poignant statue of the young Portuguese singer Luiza Todi, an archway leads into an extensive pedestrian area where many stores afford shopping and browsing adventures.

Las Ramblas is the main thoroughfare of "old" Setúbal. Look for the modern Maidens' Fountain in the center of Las Ramblas, cross over and enter a small square. Have lunch or an apéritif at an outside cafe, watch the passing parade, and gaze across at the Manueline door of the Church of São Julião.

Make a special effort to find Church of Jesus, a few blocks north of Avenida Luiza Todi on Praça Miguel Bombarda. Believed to have been the first building featuring Manueline architecture, it was designed by Boytac and built in 1491. It is very narrow with a high arched ceiling. Columns resembling twisted ropes rise to support the vaults. Side walls are decorated with pictorial *azulejos*, framed with escalloped tiles.

Among harbor scenes to be enjoyed are raucous fish auctions, meticulous and laborious mending of nets, outdoor swap meets, and oceangoing vessels disgorging catches ranging from three-inch fish to great, life-sustaining cod.

Troia Peninsula once held a Roman city built on Phoenician foundations. Destroyed by a tidal wave in the fifth century, Troia remained a wilderness until the last few years. Now it is undergoing a building boom and becoming a city again, a city of highrise apartment complexes. It is not recommended as a tourist sight unless you want to take a short boat or Hovercraft ride. Just walk along the waterfront until you locate the correct departure gate.

Pousada do Castelo de Palmela

2950 PALMELA

CH govt. rating
27 rooms
Phone (Lisboa) 235 04 10
Telex 42290

DIRECTIONS: 8 km north of Setúbal.

Adaptation and reconstruction of monastic buildings resulted in elegant Pousada do Castelo de Palmela, inaugurated in 1979. Guest rooms are quite large, with twin beds,
two leather occasional chairs with contemporary table, desk,
and hassock. Windows have a magnificent view of Setúbal
and beyond. There is a thermostat for air conditioning in
the room, and adequate lighting for reading at night.

Ends of long marble hallways and public rooms are fit-
ted with groups of antique, modern, and regional furniture. Glass-enclosed cloisters built around a gardened
courtyard are used for breakfast, bar overflow, and for
lounging. All areas are beautified by potted plants. The
Portuguese do have green thumbs. The size, variety, and
quality of coleas make an amateur horticulturist envious.

The pousada dining room is so popular with Lisbonites
that reservations should be made when checking in. In a
salon leading to the dining hall, notice a stone font used
for centuries by monks. One wall of the oblong dining
room, once the refectory of the monastery, is covered with
three outsized sketches of a stag hunt, a banquet, and a
wild boar hunt. And indeed venison and wild boar appear
on the extensive menu of traditional Portuguese and continental dishes. Chateaubriand, tournedo bearnaise, and
grilled steaks can be ordered a la carte as can *salada espe-
cial*, a green salad with tomatoes, watercress, and red cabbage. It is tossed tableside with a flair by the maitre d'.

Entrees, well prepared and expertly served, include *galinha guisada com vinho de Palmela* (chicken stewed in Palmela wine), *filetes de garoupa com salada* (grouper filets with
salad), *pataniscas de bacalhau com arroz à pousada* (codfish cakes

with green rice), *filetes de linguado com molho espumante* (filet of sole with champagne sauce), and *lombo de vaca assado em pau de louro* (sirloin on a spit). Four appetizers to consider are *figos com presunto* (figs with smoked ham), *cocktail de melão com vinho do Porto* (melon with Port), *sopa rica de peixe e marisco* (seafood soup), and *salada de tamboril com camarão* (frog legs and shrimp salad). The dessert cart is tantalizing, with a wide assortment of sweets, fruit, and cheese. Order your favorite Portuguese wine or, if you haven't by now, do try a *branco* or *tinto* Frangoneiro.

TOURING PALMELA. During a stay at the Palmela pousada, one becomes intensely aware of historical events that occurred on this very hilly spot. In the eighth century Palmela was taken by the Moors, who constructed a castle-fortress on this same high point. Afonso Henriques captured the castle in 1147 and completed reconquest of the whole area in 1165. He began castle reconstruction and founded a monastery dedicated to the Order of Santiago in 1172. In 1384, Nuno Alvares Pereira, returning victorious from the Alentejo wars, signaled the Master of Avis (soon to be João I) from castle ramparts. He assured João, under Castilian siege in Lisboa, that he would soon be on his way to help.

Work on the monastery began in 1423 and it was completed in 1482. Two years later João II, in Alcácer do Sal about to return to Lisboa via the Sado River, escaped ambush by traveling overland. When he discovered that the bishop of Evora was the instigator of the plot, he had him imprisoned in a dungeon in the keep of Palmela castle where he lasted only a few days.

The earthquake of 1755 damaged the castle but monks continued to reside in the monastery until the abolition of religious orders in 1834. Partial restoration of the castle, declared a national monument, was undertaken in 1940.

In the former monastery church near the pousada is the tomb of Jorge de Lencastre, last grand master of the Order of Santiago, son of João II, and grandson of Philippa of Lancaster. Take a stroll along the castle ramparts. On a clear day there is a 360-degree vista of the Serra da Arrábida, Castelo de São Filipe, harbor of Setúbal, pencil-thin Troia Peninsula, immobile windmills on slopes above the village of Palmela, Lisboa, and the mountains of Sintra.

Take time to look into Saint Peter's Church at the foot

of the castle hill. The interior is lined with *azulejos* showing momentous scenes in the life of Saint Peter.

Wine harvest festivities of Palmela are held from the third to the fifth of September. Activities include a procession of wine harvesters, symbolic treading of grapes, blessing of the first must, and display and tasting of wines. Also on the agenda is a running of the bulls, folk singing, and dancing, climaxed on the final night with a brilliant barrage of fireworks.

Side trips can be made to Sesimbra, a fishing village of steep narrow alleys leading to a fine beach with gentle breakers, and to Azeitão for a tour through the Fonseca winery. The modern home of Lancers is open 9–11:30 A.M. and 2–5 P.M.

The highest road in Portugal, from Manteigas to Covilhã, crosses desolate terrain.

RECOMMENDED ITINERARIES

We hope these recommended itineraries will be helpful to you in planning your trip to Spain and Portugal. We have driven the routes following Firestone-Hispania road map number P-41-42. These itineraries are designed so that you won't spend all day adding up kilometers, and we have tried to limit driving time to a maximum of four to six hours a day. When planning your journey, try to avoid a long drive on the first day.

You will notice that we have not designated stops at all the pousadas and paradores. This is not because we find certain ones less desirable—they were simply not as practical for these particular itineraries.

As a general rule, count on averaging 75 to 100 km per hour on major highways (wide red routes on the Firestone map), 120 km per hour on the freeways (*autopistas* in Spain, *autostradas* in Portugal—wide red with a yellow strip down the middle), and 60 to 80 km per hour on most secondary roads (narrow yellow and red). Never hesitate to deviate a bit and travel a secondary road, for it may be on just such a road that you will see unforgettable sights. Remember to maintain at least enough fuel to travel 100 km at all times.

"Early start" in these itineraries means checking out of your lodgings by 9 A.M. "Late arrival" means arriving in the afternoon (by 5 P.M.). Late arrival should be indicated when making reservations. If you can't make it by 5, try to telephone ahead.

Page numbers in parentheses refer to *Paradores of Spain* when in Spain and *Pousadas of Portugal* when in Portugal.

When on the road, we usually snacked midday on cheese, bread and crackers, wine, and fruit. We enjoyed browsing in village markets and shops, keeping our travel larder stocked. Tuck in a corkscrew and kitchen knife when packing. Always keep bottled water in the car.

If a stop en route to a parador or pousada is suggested, do take time for a look around or a snack.

Since we believe that half the fun of any trip comes from anticipation and planning, we have included an enlarged map of Iberia, giving locations of major cities, paradores, and pousadas, so that you may plot your own course.

Buen viaje! Boa viagem!

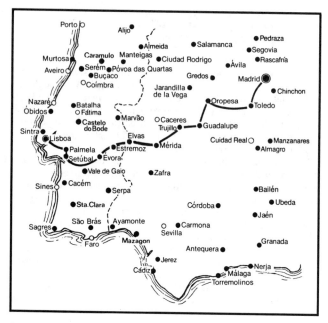

Itinerary 1

ITINERARY 1
7 days, Lisboa to Madrid or vice versa

Day 1, Lisboa to Setúbal (50 km). Leave Lisboa southeast with a stop in Palmela (p. 119) en route to Setúbal (p. 116). *Pousada de São Filipe.*

Day 2, Setúbal to Evora (100 km). Take E-4 northeast to Montemor-o-Novo, southeast on N-114 to Evora (p. 102). *Pousada dos Lóios.*

Day 3, Evora to Estremoz (49 km). Spend most of the day seeing Evora, the Museum of Portugal, before driving northeast to Estremoz (p. 98). *Pousada da Rainha Santa Isabel.*

Day 4, Estremoz to Mérida (125 km). Early start from Estremoz southeast through Borba 5 km to Vila Viçosa (p. 100) for a tour of the palace. Retrace to Borba then east through Elvas (p. 96) and Badajoz to Mérida (p. 142). *Parador Nacional Via de la Plata.*

Day 5, Mérida to Trujillo (90 km). Spend most of the day seeing Mérida's Roman ruins before leaving for Trujillo (p. 145) northeast on N-V. *Parador Nacional de Trujillo.*

NOTE: Page numbers following Spanish locales refer to *Paradores of Spain;* page numbers following Portuguese locales refer to *Pousadas of Portugal.*

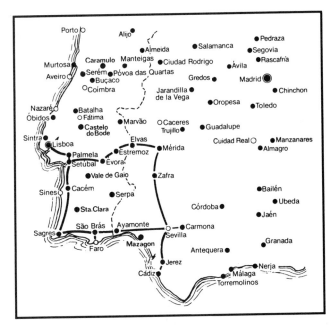

Itinerary 2

Day 6, Trujillo to Guadalupe (82 km). Drive southeast on C- 524 and at Zorita turn left onto C-401 to Guadalupe (p. 139). Twisting secondary roads, but lots of scenery. *Parador Nacional Zurbarán*.

Day 7, Guadalupe to Toledo (205 km via Oropesa). Leave Guadalupe east then head north through Puerto de San Vicente for a stop in Oropesa (p. 85). Leave E-4 at Santa Olalla, head southeast on N-403 to Toledo (p. 89). *Parador Nacional Conde de Orgaz*.

Most of the next day can be spent in Toledo, 70 km southwest of Madrid.

ITINERARY 2
10 days, round trip from Lisboa

Day 1, Lisboa to Evora (158 km). Drive southeast through Setúbal to Evora (p. 102). If interested in purchasing a *tapête*, stop in Arraiolos en route. Try to save several hours for Evora. *Pousada dos Lóios*.

NOTE: Page numbers following Spanish locales refer to *Paradores of Spain*; page numbers following Portuguese locales refer to *Pousadas of Portugal*.

Day 2, Evora to Estremoz (48 km). Budget your day to spend four or five hours visiting the environs of Estremoz (p. 98). Drive 18 km southeast through Borba to Vila Viçosa (p. 100). Take a tour of the palace and a stroll through the old town before checking into the pousada. *Pousada da Rainha Santa Isabel.*

Day 3, Estremoz to Zafra (186 km). Early start from Estremoz. Head east through Elvas (p. 96) and Badajoz to Mérida (p. 142). Spend several hours seeing the Roman ruins and perhaps have lunch at the parador. It's a one-hour drive south to Zafra (p. 147). *Late arrival. Parador Nacional Hernán Cortés.*

Day 4, Zafra to Carmona (170 km). Early start south from Zafra to Sevilla (p. 56). Follow signs to Catedral, park nearby, and take your own walking tour. Specify *late arrival* in Carmona (p. 41), 33 km east of Sevilla. *Parador Nacional Alcázar del Rey Don Pedro.*

Day 5, Carmona to Cádiz (126 km). Early start from Carmona back through Sevilla, where you pick up the *autopista* to Cádiz (p. 39). *Hotel Atlántico.*

Day 6, Cádiz to Arcos de la Frontera (70 km). Go northeast on IV to Jerez (p. 37) for a visit to one or more *bodegas* before proceeding west on C-342 to Arcos (p. 36). *Parador Nacional Casa del Corregidor.*

Day 7, Arcos de la Frontera to Ayamonte (247 km). Leave Arcos east on C-342, then go northwest on C-343, north on the *autopista* A-4 to Sevilla. Leave Sevilla west on N-431 to Ayamonte (p. 37). *Parador Nacional Costa de la Luz.*

Day 8, Ayamonte to São Brás de Alportel (44 km). Ferry from Ayamonte to Vila Real, then 22 km to Tavira, where you will turn northwest onto N-270 to São Brás (p. 107). Time to visit Faro (p. 108) if you wish. *Pousada de São Brás.*

Day 9, São Brás to Sagres (140 km). Lovely drive along the Algarve to Sagres (p. 110). Try to arrive for 3:30 daily movie (in English) about Prince Henry. *Pousada do Infante.*

Day 10, Sagres to Santiago do Cacém (137 km) or Sagres to Setúbal (237 km) or Sagres to Palmela (243 km). Drive north to Santiago do Cacém (p. 114) for lunch and go on to Setúbal or Palmela, or spend the night in Santiago do Cacém. *Pousada de São Tiago, Santiago do Cacém. Pousada de São Filipe, Setúbal. Pousada de Palmela, Palmela.*

50 km to Lisboa from Setúbal or 150 km to Lisboa from Santiago.

ITINERARY 3
8 days, round trip from Lisboa

Day 1, Lisboa to Batalha (148 km). Drive north on E-3 then onto N-1. Cut west 28 km for stop in Obidos (p. 41), go through Caldas

---

NOTE: Page numbers following Spanish locales refer to *Paradores of Spain;* page numbers following Portuguese locales refer to *Pousadas of Portugal.*

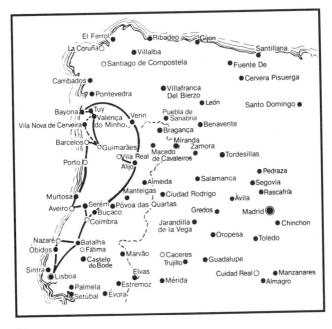

Itinerary 3

da Rainha for stop in Alcobaça (p. 45) and on to Nazaré (p. 43) for visit of two or three hours, perhaps including lunch. Arrive in Batalha (p. 47) for late afternoon visit to monastery. *Pousada do Mestre Afonso Domingues.*

Day 2, Batalha to Murtosa (183 km). Leave Batalha driving north on N-1 through Leiria and Coimbra (p. 53). At Santo António Agueda, cut west to Aveiro (p. 64) for visit of two or three hours. Drive east from Aveiro and cut north at Angeja, through Estarreja to Murtosa (p. 63). *Pousada da Ria.*

Day 3, Murtosa to Guimarães (115 km). If it's Thursday, you will want to head for Barcelos's market (p. 68), skirting Porto. Or you can visit Porto (p. 65) for several hours, then head for Guimarães (p. 67). Might be wise to specify *late arrival* in any case. *Pousada Santa Maria da Oliveira or Pousada Santa Marinha da Costa.*

Day 4, Guimarães to Valença do Minho or Vila Nova de Cerveira (92 km). Drive north from Guimarães for a visit to Braga (p. 70). The area from Ponte de Lima to Ponte da Barca has several *solares,* manor houses, you might want to visit. Get a list from the Por-

---

NOTE: Page numbers following Spanish locales refer to *Paradores of Spain;* page numbers following Portuguese locales refer to *Pousadas of Portugal.*

tuguese National Tourist Office before leaving home. Stay either in Vila Nova (p. 73) or Valença (p. 75). *Pousada de Dom Dinis or Pousada de São Teotónio.*

Day 5, Valença do Minho or Vila Nova de Cerveira to Bayona (60 km). Enjoy morning hours in Valença before crossing international bridge into Spain at Tuy (p. 162). Get pesetas at border bank. Leave Tuy driving southwest through Laguardia before arriving in Bayona (p. 152). *Parador Nacional Conde de Gondomar.*

Day 6, Bayona to Verin (205 km). Beautiful drive through southern Galicia and Orense, then southeast to Verin (p. 164). *Parador Nacional Monterrey.*

Day 7, Verin to Alijó (136 km). Drive south from Verin into Portugal. In autumn, you will see wonderful grape harvest scenes if you drive southeast from Chaves through Valpacos and Mirandela, then southwest on N-15 before turning south to Alijó (p. 82). *Pousada Barão de Forrester.*

Day 8, Alijó to Buçaco (224 km). Travel west to Vila Real and Highway N-2, south through Viseu (p. 92) to Buçaco (p. 56). *Palace Hotel.*

231 km south from Buçaco to Lisboa.

ITINERARY 4
8 days, Lisboa to Madrid or vice versa

Day 1, Lisboa to Batalha (148 km). Drive north on E-3 then onto N-1. Cut west on Highway 366 for a stop in Obidos (p. 41), through Caldas da Rainha to Highway 8 for a stop in Alcobaça (p. 45) and on to Nazaré (p. 43) for two or three hours' visit and perhaps lunch. Arrive in Batalha (p. 47) for late afternoon visit to monastery. *Pousada do Mestre Afonso Domingues.*

Day 2, Batalha to Buçaco (110 km). Two choices of sights en route to Buçaco. EITHER leave Batalha heading southeast and go 13 km for a visit to Fátima (p. 49). Tomar (p. 51) is 31 km southeast of Fátima. Leave Tomar north on N-110 through Penela and cut over to N-1 at Condeixa for a stop in Conímbriga (p. 53), on through Coimbra to Buçaco (p. 56). OR bypass Fátima and Tomar and head directly for Coimbra (p. 53) for a visit of several hours. Take N-1 north to Highway 234, east to Luso, then follow signs to Buçaco (p. 56). *Palace Hotel.*

Day 3, Buçaco to Valença do Minho or Vila Nova de Cerveira (245 km). If it's Thursday, get an early start north to Barcelos (p. 68) for its market. If not, you may opt to spend several hours in Porto (p. 65) before proceeding north to Valença (p. 75) or Vila Nova de Cerveira (p. 73). *Pousada de São Teotónio or Pousada de Dom Dinis.*

NOTE: Page numbers following Spanish locales refer to *Paradores of Spain;* page numbers following Portuguese locales refer to *Pousadas of Portugal.*

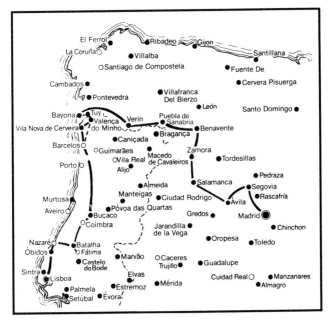

Itinerary 4

Day 4, *Valença do Minho or Vila Nova de Cerveira to Bayona (60 km).* Enjoy the morning in Valença before crossing the international bridge into Spain at Tuy (p. 162). Remember to buy pesetas at the border bank. You may want to stroll through Tuy before driving northwest to Bayona (p. 152). *Parador Nacional Conde de Gondomar.*

Day 5, *Bayona to Verin (205 km).* Beautiful drive through southern Galicia and Orense, then southeast to Verin (p. 164). *Parador Nacional Monterrey.*

Day 6, *Verin to Zamora (240 km).* Drive east through Puebla de Sanabria (p. 106). Stop in Benavente (p. 94) before continuing south to Zamora (p. 119). *Parador Nacional Condes de Alba y Aliste.*

Day 7, *Zamora to Avila (162 km).* Plan a visit of two to three hours in Salamanca (p. 106), 62 km south of Zamora, before continuing southeast to Avila (p. 93). *Parador Nacional Raimundo de Borgoña.*

Day 8, *Avila to Segovia (65 km).* Divide your day between Avila and Segovia (p. 113). *Parador Nacional de Segovia.*

88 km to Madrid.

NOTE: Page numbers following Spanish locales refer to *Paradores of Spain;* page numbers following Portuguese locales refer to *Pousadas of Portugal.*

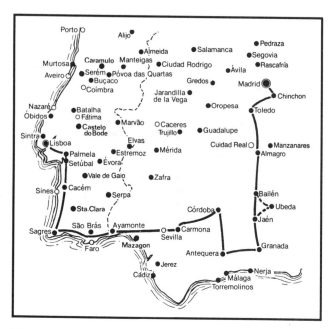

Itinerary 5

10 days, Lisboa to Madrid or vice versa

Day 1, Lisboa to Santiago do Cacém (150 km). Drive southeast to Setúbal (p. 116) or Palmela (p. 119) for a visit, then on to Santiago do Cacém (p. 114). *Pousada de São Tiago.*

Day 2, Santiago do Cacém to Sagres (137 km). Easy drive south and spend most of the afternoon in Sagres (p. 110). *Pousada do Infante.*

Day 3, Sagres to Ayamonte (180 km). Interesting drive east along the Algarve to Vila Real, where you ferry into Spain at Ayamonte (p. 37). *Parador Nacional Costa de la Luz.*

Day 4, Ayamonte to Carmona (186 km). Early start from Ayamonte through Huelva to Sevilla (p. 56). Follow signs to Catedral, park nearby, and take walking tour of Sevilla's monuments. Specify *late arrival* in Carmona (p. 41), 33 km east of Sevilla. *Parador Nacional Alcázar del Rey Don Pedro.*

Day 5, Carmona to Córdoba (105 km). Short drive, allowing several hours of sightseeing in Córdoba (p. 44). *Parador Nacional La Arruzafa.*

NOTE: Page numbers following Spanish locales refer to *Paradores of Spain;* page numbers following Portuguese locales refer to *Pousadas of Portugal.*

Day 6, Córdoba to Granada (229 km). Drive south to Antequera
(p. 33), then east to Granada (p. 47). *Parador Nacional San Francisco
or, if no vacancy, Alhambra Palace Hotel.*

Day 7. A full day for sightseeing in Granada. *Parador Nacional San
Francisco.*

Day 8, Granada to Almagro (267 km). You may want to stop for a
morning coffee break at the spectacular parador in Jaén (p. 49), or
take time for a visit to Ubeda (p. 57). Either way, specify *late arrival* in Almagro (p. 77). *Parador Nacional de Almagro.*

Day 9, Almagro to Toledo (139 km). Leave Almagro east and drive
to C-517, then head north on N-420 to N-IV and Madridejos,
northwest on C-400 to Toledo (p. 89). *Parador Nacional Conde de
Orgaz.*

Day 10, Toledo to Chinchón (66 km). Most of the day for shopping
and sightseeing in Toledo before departing northeast to Chinchón
(p. 79). *Parador Nacional de Chinchón.*

33 km northwest to Madrid.

ITINERARY 6
13 days, round trip from Madrid

Day 1, Madrid to Toledo (70 km). Drive southwest on N-401 to Toledo (p. 89). *Parador Nacional Conde de Orgaz.*

Day 2, Toledo to Guadalupe (205 km). Drive northwest 47 km and
join N-V at Santa Olalla. Stop in Oropesa (p. 85). Proceed southwest to Guadalupe (p. 139). You might consider having dinner at
the monastery across the street from the parador. *Parador Nacional
Zurbarán.*

Day 3, Guadalupe to Mérida (130 km). Leave Guadalupe southwest
on C-401, then N-V to Mérida (p. 142). *Parador Nacional Via de la
Plata.*

Day 4, Mérida to Estremoz (135 km). Drive west through Badajoz
and Elvas (p. 96). At Borba, cut southeast 5 km to Vila Viçosa
(p. 100) for visit of two or three hours before proceeding to Estremoz (p. 98). *Pousada da Rainha Santa Isabel.*

Day 5, Estremoz to Evora (69 km via Arraiolos). If interested in purchasing a *tapête*, leave Estremoz driving west to Arraiolos, then
21 km southeast to Evora (p. 102). *Pousada dos Lóios.*

Day 6. Another day for sightseeing in Evora. *Pousada dos Lóios.*

Day 7, Evora to Lisboa (158 km). Early start for a visit to Setúbal
(p. 116) and Palmela (p. 119) before arrival in Lisboa (p. 28).

Days 8 and 9, Lisboa.

NOTE: Page numbers following Spanish locales refer to *Paradores
of Spain;* page numbers following Portuguese locales refer to *Pousadas of Portugal.*

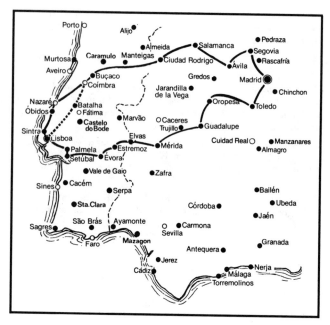

Itinerary 6

Day 10, Lisboa to Buçaco (231 km). Get an early start. Choose between two routes: EITHER Sintra (p. 35), Mafra (p. 39), Nazaré (p. 43), Alcobaça (p. 45), and on to Buçaco (p. 56). OR drive the *autostrada* north for stops in Batalha (p. 47), Conímbriga (p. 53), and Coimbra (p. 53), and on to Buçaco. *Palace Hotel.*

Day 11, Buçaco to Ciudad Rodrigo (214 km). Head east on Highway 234 to N-16, through Guarda (p. 91), cross into Spain at Fuentes de Oñoro and on to Ciudad Rodrigo (p. 98). *Parador Nacional Enrique II.*

Day 12, Ciudad Rodrigo to Avila (189 km). Leave Ciudad Rodrigo northeast on E-3. Stop for visit in Salamanca (p. 106) before continuing to Avila (p. 93). *Parador Nacional Raimundo de Borgoña.*

Day 13, Avila to Segovia (65 km). Allow most of the day for the sights of Avila before driving to Segovia (p. 113). *Parador Nacional de Segovia.*

88 km to Madrid.

NOTE: Page numbers following Spanish locales refer to *Paradores of Spain;* page numbers following Portuguese locales refer to *Pousadas of Portugal.*

ITINERARY 7
15 days, Barcelona to Lisboa or vice versa (central route)

Day 1, Barcelona to Tortosa (193 km). Drive south via the Barcelona-Valencia *autopista*. Take the Tortosa exit 14 km north through the Ebro valley to Tortosa (p. 130). *Parador Nacional Castillo de la Zuda.*

Day 2, Tortosa to Alcañiz (91 km). Take your choice of secondary roads northwest to Alcañiz (p. 64). *Parador Nacional La Concordia.*

Day 3, Alcañiz to Sigüenza (252 km). A day of winding secondary roads but you will have Day 4 to rest. Leave Alcañiz south on N-211 to Caminreal, south then west on N-211, now a principal highway, to Alcolea del Pinar, then northwest on C-114 to Sigüenza (p. 87). *Parador Nacional Castillo de Sigüenza.*

Day 4. A day of relaxation, with possible trips to Santa María de Huerta (p. 108) and Medinaceli (p. 109), besides a stroll through Sigüenza. *Parador Nacional Castillo de Sigüenza.*

Day 5, Sigüenza to Segovia (236 km). Leave Sigüenza south on C-204, then pick up E-4. If you wish to avoid Madrid, take the airport freeway north past the airport, through Alcobendas, across N-1 to C-601, north and west through Navacerrada, and north on N-601 to Segovia (p. 113). *Parador Nacional de Segovia.*

Day 6, Segovia. Visit La Granja and have lunch at Hostería Nacional Pintor Zuloaga in Pedraza (p. 104). *Parador Nacional de Segovia.*

Day 7, Segovia to Madrid. Leave you car and luggage at the parador and take the train into Madrid (p. 81). There are many trains daily arriving and departing both Atocha and Chamartín stations. A convenient hotel is the Chamartín (p. 82).

Days 8 and 9, Madrid.

Day 10, Madrid to Avila. Take the train back to Segovia, pick up luggage and car, and head southwest to Avila (p. 93). *Parador Nacional Raimundo de Borgoña.*

Day 11, Avila to Ciudad Rodrigo (189 km). Drive northwest on N-501 for stop in Salamanca (p. 106) en route to Ciudad Rodrigo (p. 98). *Parador Nacional Enrique II.*

Day 12, Ciudad Rodrigo to Manteigas (135 km). Cross into Portugal at Fuentes de Oñoro, go through Guarda (p. 91), following signs to Covilhã. Take N-18 south for 27 km and turn west on 232 to Manteigas (p. 90). It's another 12 km to the pousada. *Pousada de São Lourenço.*

Day 13, Manteigas to Buçaco (156 km). Leave the pousada heading north through Gouveia, pick up N-17, head southeast to Poiares,

---

NOTE: Page numbers following Spanish locales refer to *Paradores of Spain;* page numbers following Portuguese locales refer to *Pousadas of Portugal.*

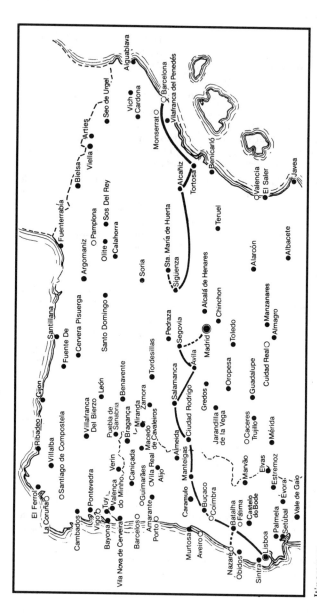

Itinerary 7

northeast on Highway 2 for 13 km, and pick up signs to Buçaco (p. 56). *Palace Hotel.*

Day 14, Buçaco to Batalha (110 km). After morning hours enjoying the environs of the Palace Hotel, drive south to Coimbra (p. 53) for a visit of two or three hours before proceeding south to Batalha (p. 47). *Pousada do Mestre Afonso Domingues.*

Day 15. Another day based in Batalha for trips of your choice: Tomar (p. 51), Fátima (p. 49), Nazaré (p. 43). *Pousada do Mestre Afonso Domingues.*

148 km to Lisboa.

ITINERARY 8
15 days, Galician tour from Lisboa to Madrid or vice versa

Day 1, Lisboa to Batalha (148 km). Drive north on E-3 then onto N-1. Cut west 28 km for stop in Obidos (p. 41), through Caldas da Rainha for a stop in Alcobaça (p. 45) and on to Nazaré (p. 43) for visit of two to three hours, perhaps lunch. Arrive in Batalha (p. 47) for late afternoon visit to monastery. *Pousada do Mestre Afonso Domingues.*

Day 2, Batalha to Murtosa (183 km). Leave Batalha driving north on N-1 through Leiria and stop in Coimbra (p. 53) for two-hour visit. Leave Coimbra north on N-1. At Santo António Agueda, cut west to Aveiro (p. 64) for two-hour stop. Drive east from Aveiro and cut north at Angeja to go through Estarreja to Murtosa (p. 63). *Pousada da Ria.*

Day 3, Murtosa to Valença do Minho or Vila Nova de Cerveira (200 km via Porto or 237 km via Barcelos). If it's Thursday, drive north, skirting Porto, through Guimarães (p. 67) and Braga (p. 70) for the market in Barcelos (p. 68). Or you may choose to visit Porto (p. 65) for a couple of hours before driving north on N-13 to Vila Nova or Valença. They are 12 km apart. *Pousada de São Teotónio or Pousada de Dom Dinis.*

Day 4, Valença do Minho or Vila Nova de Cerveira to Bayona (60 km). Enjoy morning hours in Valença (p. 75) before crossing international bridge into Spain at Tuy (p. 162). Get pesetas at border bank. Leave Tuy driving southwest through Laguardia for spectacular scenery before arriving in Bayona (p. 152). *Parador Nacional Conde de Gondomar.*

Day 5, Bayona to Cambados (88 km). Leisurely day along the scenic rías (estuaries) of Galicia; go through Vigo and Pontevedra (p. 157) to Cambados (p. 154). *Parador Nacional del Albariño.*

NOTE: Page numbers following Spanish locales refer to *Paradores of Spain;* page numbers following Portuguese locales refer to *Pousadas of Portugal.*

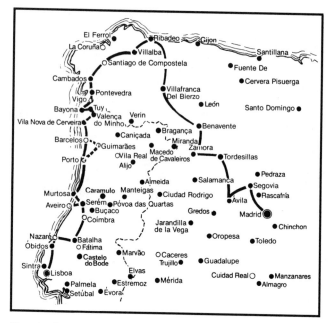

Itinerary 8

Day 6, Cambados to Santiago de Compostela (82 km). Easy drive north to Santiago (p. 159), allowing most of the day for this exciting, historic city. *Hotel Reyes Católicos.*

Day 7, Santiago de Compostela to Villalba (92 km). Try for one of the six rooms at the parador in Villalba (p. 165). If unsuccessful, spend another night in Santiago. There is plenty to do and see. *Parador Nacional Condes de Villalba.*

Day 8, Villalba to Ribadeo (73 km). Leave Villalba northeast on N-643 for Ribadeo (p. 158). You may want to check into parador before exploring small nearby coastal villages. *Parador Nacional de Ribadeo.*

Day 9, Ribadeo to Villafranca del Bierzo (190 km). Drive south on N-640 through Lugo then onto N-VI to Villafranca (p. 118). *Parador Nacional Villafranca del Bierzo.*

Day 10, Villafranca to Zamora (215 km). Drive southeast on N-VI to Benavente (p. 94) for lunch before continuing to Zamora (p. 119). *Parador Nacional Condes Alba y Aliste.*

NOTE: Page numbers following Spanish locales refer to *Paradores of Spain;* page numbers following Portuguese locales refer to *Pousadas of Portugal.*

Day 11, Zamora to Tordesillas (67 km). Spend the rest of the day and days 12 and 13 in the area around Tordesillas (p. 116). Take a castle tour of your own (p. 117), returning each night to the very comfortable parador. *Parador Nacional de Tordesillas.*

Days 12 and 13, Tordesillas. Parador Nacional de Tordesillas.

Day 14, Tordesillas to Avila (136 km). You will have most of the day for the sights of Avila (p. 93) if you get an early start from Tordesillas. *Parador Nacional Raimundo de Borgoña.*

Day 15, Avila to Segovia (65 km). Early start from Avila for many hours in Segovia (p. 113). *Parador Nacional de Segovia.*

88 km to Madrid.

ITINERARY 9
15 days, coastal trip from Barcelona to Lisboa or vice versa

Day 1, Barcelona to Tortosa (193 km). Leave Barcelona heading south on either the *autopista* or N-340 to Vilafranca del Penedés (p. 133) for a visit to the wine museum. Then continue to Tortosa (p. 130). There is a Tortosa exit from the *autopista*. *Parador Nacional Castillo de la Zuda.*

Day 2, Tortosa to El Saler (194 km). Rejoin the *autopista* for drive south through Castellón and Valencia to El Saler (p. 174). Plenty of time for a game of golf. *Parador Nacional Luis Vives.*

Day 3. Another day for a visit to Valencia. *Parador Nacional Luis Vives.*

Day 4, El Saler to Javea (119 km). Leisurely day to enjoy beautiful surroundings of Javea (p. 177), southeast of El Saler. *Parador Nacional Costa Blanca.*

Day 5, Jávea to Mojácar (207 km). Drive southwest on the *autopista* to Alicante then take N-340 to Puerto Lumbreras (p. 86) for lunch and perhaps a stop at the parador. At Vera, travel south on C-323 to Mojácar (p. 53). *Parador Nacional Reyes Católicos.*

Day 6, Mojácar to Nerja (278 km). Rejoin N-340 south to Almería. If it's lunchtime, stop at the Club de Mar Restaurant in Almería (p. 54). Drive along the Mediterranean to Nerja (p. 54). *Parador Nacional de Nerja.*

Day 7, Nerja to Torremolinos (70 km). Easy drive with plenty of time to stop off in Málaga (p. 50) for lunch at the Gibralfaro parador. On to Torremolinos (p. 59). *Parador Nacional del Golf.*

Day 8. A day in Torremolinos for golf or an excursion to Mijas, Casares (p. 60), or Ronda. *Parador Nacional del Golf.*

NOTE: Page numbers following Spanish locales refer to *Paradores of Spain;* page numbers following Portuguese locales refer to *Pousadas of Portugal.*

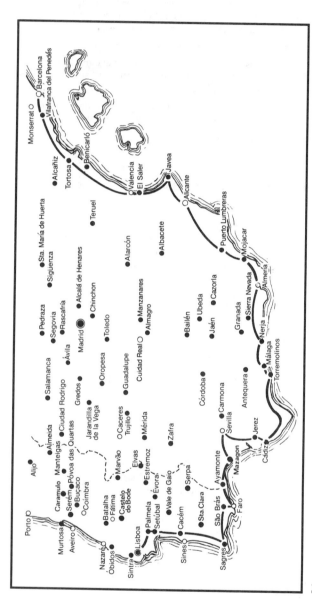

Itinerary 9

Day 9, Torremolinos to Cádiz (244 km). A day of exceptional scenery along coastal Highway N-340 as you round the southern tip of Spain and head northwest to Cádiz (p. 39). *Hotel Atlántico.*

Day 10, Cádiz to Mazagón (211 km). A rather roundabout route to Mazagón. You may want to stop in Jerez (p. 37) to visit a *bodega* or two before traveling the *autopista* to Sevilla, then west on 334, turning south just before reaching San Juan del Puerto to Mazagón (p. 51). *Parador Nacional Cristóbal Colón.*

Day 11. Another day for Mazagón as a base while you see sights of the Coto de Doñana (p. 52). *Parador Nacional Cristóbal Colón.*

Day 12, Mazagón to São Brás de Alportel (147 km via Faro). Drive northwest to Huelva to pick up N-IV at Ayamonte (p. 37), where you will ferry into Portugal at Vila Real de Santo António. Drive south for a look at Faro (p. 108) before turning north and going 18 km to São Brás (p. 107). *Pousada de São Brás de Alportel.*

Day 13, São Brás de Alportel to Sagres (140 km). Leave São Brás west to Loulé, then 13 more km to join N-125, the coastal route. You will have time for many stops. Albufeira is a quaint fishing village with many stores to shop. Lagos (p. 112) is another such town. From there, just 43 km to Sagres (p. 110). *Pousada do Infante.*

Day 14, Sagres to Setúbal or Palmela (216 km). This looks like a long haul on the map but it is an easy drive. Stop in Santiago do Cacém (p. 114) for lunch at the pousada before continuing to Setúbal (p. 116) or Palmela (p. 119). *Pousada de São Filipe or Pousada de Palmela.*

Day 15, Setúbal, Palmela, and environs. Visit the Fonseca winery in Azeitão (p. 121) or explore Sesimbra (p. 121). *Pousada de São Filipe or Pousada de Palmela.*

50 km to Lisboa.

ITINERARY 10
22 days, round trip from Lisboa

Day 1, Lisboa to Obidos (149 km). Stop in Sintra (p. 35) and lunch at Hotel Palácio dos Seteais before driving north to Mafra (p. 39), then on to Obidos (p. 41). *Pousada do Castelo.*

Day 2, Obidos to Batalha (72 km). Leave Obidos driving north through Caldas da Rainha for a stop in Alcobaça (p. 45) before proceeding 13 km northwest to Nazaré (p. 43) for a visit and lunch. It's 26 km to Batalha (p. 47). *Pousada do Mestre Afonso Domingues.*

Day 3. Another day based in Batalha to allow trips to Fátima (p. 49) and Tomar (p. 51). *Pousada do Mestre Afonso Domingues.*

NOTE: Page numbers following Spanish locales refer to *Paradores of Spain;* page numbers following Portuguese locales refer to *Pousadas of Portugal.*

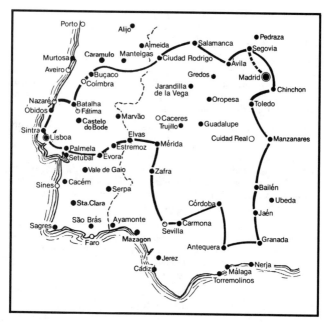

Itinerary 10

Day 4, Batalha to Buçaco (110 km). Leave Batalha driving north on N-1 with a brief stop in Conímbriga (p. 53) and three to four hours in Coimbra (p. 53) before proceeding northeast to Buçaco (p. 56). *Palace Hotel.*

Day 5, Buçaco to Ciudad Rodrigo (217 km). Leave Buçaco heading east a few kilometers before turning south at Santa Comba Dão onto N-234 then northeast on N-17 to pass through Guarda (p. 91). Cross into Spain at Fuentes de Oñoro and on to Ciudad Rodrigo (p. 98). *Parador Nacional Enrique II.*

Day 6, Ciudad Rodrigo to Avila (189 km). Early start from Ciudad Rodrigo to allow for several hours in Salamanca (p. 106) before proceeding to Avila (p. 93). *Parador Nacional Raimundo de Borgoña.*

Day 7, Avila to Segovia (65 km). Allow several hours for Avila before proceeding to Segovia (p. 113). *Parador Nacional de Segovia.*

Day 8, Segovia. Perhaps visit La Granja and have lunch in Pedraza (p. 104). If you don't want to drive in Madrid (p. 81), check train schedules (several a day) and make arrangements with parador to leave luggage and car. *Parador Nacional de Segovia.*

NOTE: Page numbers following Spanish locales refer to *Paradores of Spain;* page numbers following Portuguese locales refer to *Pousadas of Portugal.*

Days 9, 10, and 11, Madrid.

Day 12, Segovia to Chinchón (161 km). Early train from Madrid to Segovia. Pick up luggage and car and drive southeast to Chinchón (p. 79), skirting Madrid. Specify *late arrival. Parador Nacional de Chinchón.*

Day 13, Chinchón to Toledo (70 km). Not a long or difficult drive, allowing most of the day for Toledo (p. 89). *Parador Nacional Conde de Orgaz.*

Day 14, Toledo to Jaén (273 km). Stop off at the parador in Manzanares (p. 83) or Bailén (p. 38) for a rest or refreshment before continuing to Jaén (p. 49). *Parador Nacional Castillo Santa Catalina.*

Day 15, Jaén to Granada (97 km). Easy drive so you can have most of the day for Granada (p. 47). *Parador Nacional San Francisco.*

Day 16, Granada to Córdoba (229 km). Drive west from Granada on N-342. Have lunch at the parador in Antequera (p. 33). Then turn north on N-331 to Córdoba (p. 44). *Parador Nacional La Arruzafa.*

Day 17, Córdoba. Day to explore and rest. *Parador Nacional La Arruzafa.*

Day 18, Córdoba to Carmona (105 km). Early start, heading southwest on N-IV to Carmona (p. 41). Check into parador then take a bus into Sevilla (p. 56). *Parador Nacional Alcázar del Rey Don Pedro.*

Day 19, Carmona to Mérida (245 km). Plan to have lunch at the parador in Zafra (p. 147) en route to Mérida (p. 142). *Parador Nacional Via de la Plata.*

Day 20, Mérida. A full day to explore the ancient city. *Parador Nacional Via de la Plata.*

Day 21, Mérida to Estremoz (124 km). You will have time to stop en route for a visit to Vila Viçosa (p. 100) before arriving in Estremoz (p. 98). *Pousada da Rainha Santa Isabel.*

Day 22, Estremoz to Palmela (155 km). Early start to allow two or three hours in Évora (p. 102) before continuing to Palmela (p. 119). *Pousada de Palmela.*

44 km to Lisboa.

ITINERARY 11
21 days, northern route from Barcelona to Lisboa or vice versa

Day 1, Barcelona to Seo de Urgel (187 km). Leave Barcelona heading northwest through Manresa with a stop at the parador in Cardona (p. 127). At Basella, join C-1313 to Seo (p. 129). *Parador Nacional de Seo de Urgel.*

NOTE: Page numbers following Spanish locales refer to *Paradores of Spain;* page numbers following Portuguese locales refer to *Pousadas of Portugal.*

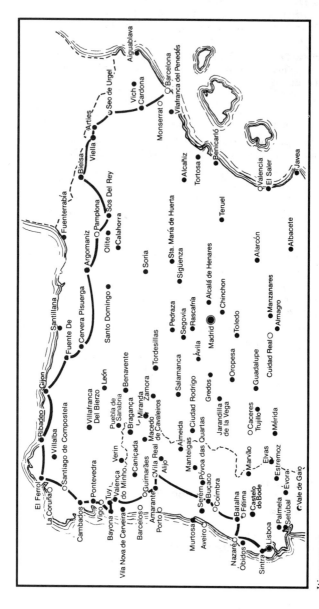

Itinerary 11

Day 2, Seo de Urgel to Viella (164 km). Backtrack south on C-1313 about 6 km and turn west onto a road appearing only on regional maps; go for 78 km in second or third gear to Sort. In any of several small towns, pick up some *queso* (cheese), *pan* (bread), and a bottle of wine so that when you reach the acme of the route (6734 feet) at Puerto de la Bonaigua you can ice the wine in roadside snow. Unforgettable lunch in the midst of the Pyrenees. Stop at the parador in Arties (p. 125) for a look around and a chat with the young administrator, who speaks English. Just a few km to Viella (p. 134). *Parador Nacional Valle de Arán.*

Day 3, Viella to Bielsa (164 km). Leave Viella via the 6-km tunnel. After you have gone 38 km look for a road west to Castejón. At Castejón, turn south then west to Ainsa. Drive north from Ainsa 34 km to Bielsa, then 14 km more west to the parador (p. 65). These roads are narrow with no center stripe—adequate, but might be a little scary in occasionally heavy summer traffic. *Parador Nacional Monte Perdido.*

Day 4, Bielsa to Sos del Rey Católico (245 km). Return to Ainsa, where you turn west on C-138 through Broto to Biescas, then south to Sabinanigo, west to Jaca, and take C-134 for about 10 km beyond Berdún. Turn south on C-137 for 34 km to Sos del Rey Católico (p. 66). A long, rather hard drive, but rewarding scenery. Watch out for herds of sheep! *Parador Nacional Fernando de Aragón.*

Day 5, Sos del Rey Católico to Argómaniz (156 km). Leave Sos del Rey Católico heading northwest through Sangüesa and in 5 km turn west onto N-240 to Pamplona (p. 182). You will have time for two or three hours in Pamplona. It is simplest to park on the outskirts of the old town and take a cab to begin a walking tour. It's 94 km to Argómaniz (p. 181). *Parador Nacional de Argómaniz.*

Day 6, Argómaniz. A day for a junket into France (remember to get francs at a border bank) or a visit to the parador in Fuenterrabía (p. 183). *Parador Nacional de Argómaniz.*

Day 7, Argómaniz to Cervera de Pisuerga (174 km). Leave Argómaniz heading through Vitoria southwest to Burgos if you wish. This route will add about 65 km. Otherwise, at Pancorbo, cut west on N-232 through Poza de la Sal and Portillo, go northwest to Aguilar de Campóo, then go 25 more km to Cervera (p. 97). *Parador Nacional Fuentes Carrionas.*

Day 8, Cervera to Fuente Dé (85 km). Drive north on C-627 then west through Potes to Fuente Dé (p. 101). Breathtaking scenery in the Picos de Europa. *Parador Nacional Río Deva.*

Day 9, Fuente Dé to Gijón (206 km). Retrace route to Potes, turn north to Panes, west on C-6312 to Cangas de Onis, and pick up N-634 west to the turn-off north to Gijón (p. 70). In Cangas de Onis, there's a Romanesque bridge over the Sella River. Used now

NOTE: Page numbers following Spanish locales refer to *Paradores of Spain;* page numbers following Portuguese locales refer to *Pousadas of Portugal.*

only for foot traffic, it is strangely humped in the middle. You are in sacred Spanish territory because it was in nearby Covadonga that tribal leader Pelayo defeated the Moors in 722. He was then made king of Asturias and established his court in Cangas. *Parador Nacional Molino Viejo.*

Day 10, Gijón to Ribadeo (156 km). Winding scenic drive west on N-632 then N-634 to Ribadeo (p. 158). *Parador Nacional de Ribadeo.*

Day 11, Ribadeo to El Ferrol (146 km via C-642 or 188 km via Villalba). Take your choice of two routes to El Ferrol (p. 156). You might enjoy seeing the parador in Villalba (p. 165). *Parador Nacional del Ferrol.*

Day 12, El Ferrol. Take a bus trip from here into La Coruña. *Parador Nacional del Ferrol.*

Day 13, El Ferrol to Santiago de Compostela (97 km). Drive north around the bay, then south on N-VI to Betanzos, south on C-542 for shortcut to N-550 and on into Santiago (p. 159). *Hotel Reyes Católicos.*

Day 14, Santiago de Compostela. Hotel Reyes Católicos.

Day 15, Santiago de Compostela to Bayona (113 km). Leave Santiago heading south on E-50 and at Puentecesures, turn southwest on C-550 for a drive and stop at parador in Cambados (p. 154), then through Sanjenjo, Pontevedra, Vigo, and the coastal road to Bayona (p. 152). *Parador Nacional Conde de Gondomar.*

Day 16, Bayona to Guimarães (128 km). Drive east through Gondomar to join N-550 and proceed to Tuy (p. 162). Cross the international bridge, remembering to stop and change money. Linger a while in Valença do Minho (p. 75), then head south through Braga (p. 70) to Guimarães (p. 67). *Pousada Santa Maria da Oliveira or Pousada Santa Marinha da Costa.*

Day 17, Guimarães to Amarante (53 km). Short drive southeast, to allow time to relax in Amarante (p. 80). *Pousada de São Gonçalo.*

Day 18, Amarante to Buçaco (204 km). Drive east to Vila Real, south on N-2 through Viseu (p. 92), through Santa Comba Dão to Buçaco (p. 56). *Palace Hotel.*

Day 19, Buçaco to Batalha (110 km). Take time for a walk through the forest before driving through Luso to pick up N-1 at Mealhada. Stop for a visit in Coimbra (p. 53). Leave Coimbra south through Condeixa for a look at Conímbriga's Roman ruins (p. 53) before arrival in Batalha (p. 47). *Pousada do Mestre Afonso Domingues.*

Day 20, Batalha and environs. Visits to Fátima (p. 49) and Tomar (p. 51). *Pousada do Mestre Afonso Domingues.*

Day 21, Batalha to Sintra (128 km). Drive from Batalha southwest to Nazaré (p. 43) for a visit, then on to Alcobaça (p. 45) for a tour

---

NOTE: Page numbers following Spanish locales refer to *Paradores of Spain;* page numbers following Portuguese locales refer to *Pousadas of Portugal.*

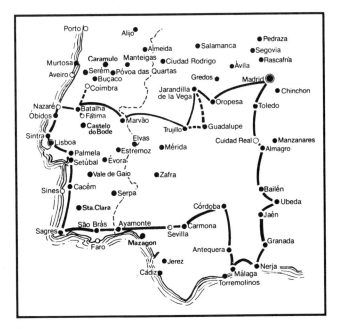

Itinerary 12

of the monastery, southwest for another monastery, at Mafra (p. 39), before arrival in Sintra (p. 35). *Hotel Palácio dos Seteais.*

Day 22, Sintra. Visit the two palaces in Sintra and the one in Queluz (p. 38), with lunch at Restaurante Cozinha Velha. *Hotel Palácio dos Seteais.*

30 km to Lisboa.

ITINERARY 12
24 days, round trip from Malaga

Day 1, Málaga to Córdoba (178 km). Drive north on N-321 with a stop in Antequera (p. 33) en route to Córdoba (p. 44). *Parador Nacional La Arruzafa.*

Day 2, Córdoba to Carmona (105 km). Spend the morning in Córdoba, then head southwest on N-IV to Carmona (p. 41). *Parador Nacional Alcázar del Rey Don Pedro.*

Day 3, Carmona. Explore Carmona, then take a bus into Sevilla (p. 56). *Parador Nacional Alcázar del Rey Don Pedro.*

NOTE: Page numbers following Spanish locales refer to *Paradores of Spain;* page numbers following Portuguese locales refer to *Pousadas of Portugal.*

Day 4, Carmona to São Brás de Alportel (230 km). Early start from Carmona west through Sevilla and Huelva to Ayamonte (p. 37), where you take a ferry to Vila Real, Portugal. At Tavira, cut north on N-270 to São Brás (p. 107). *Pousada de São Brás de Alportel.*

Day 5, São Brás de Alportel to Sagres (141 km via Faro). Enjoy a scenic drive along the Algarve west to Sagres (p. 110). *Pousada do Infante.*

Day 6, Sagres and environs. Trips to Lagos (p. 112) and Albufeira. *Pousada do Infante.*

Day 7, Sagres to Palmela (243 km). Leave Sagres north on N-120 to Santiago do Cacém (p. 114) for a rest and perhaps lunch before continuing to Palmela (p. 119). *Pousada do Castelo de Palmela.*

Day 8, Palmela to Lisboa (56 km). A leisurely day for visits to Setúbal (p. 116) and Fonseca winery in Azeitão (p. 121) before late arrival in Lisboa (p. 28).

Days 9 and 10, Lisboa.

Day 11, Lisboa to Obidos (120 km). En route to Obidos (p. 41), stop in Sintra (p. 35) and Mafra (p. 39). *Pousada do Castelo.*

Day 12, Obidos to Batalha (72 km via Nazaré). Leave Obidos heading north through Caldas da Rainha (p. 44) for visit to Alcobaça (p. 45) before continuing to Nazaré. Drive north from Nazaré 26 km to Batalha (p. 47). *Pousada do Mestre Afonso Domingues.*

Day 13, Batalha and environs. Visits to Fátima (p. 49), Tomar (p. 51), or Coimbra (p. 53). *Pousada do Mestre Afonso Domingues.*

Day 14, Batalha to Marvão (159 km). Leave Batalha heading south through Porto de Mos, Constância, Alpalhão. Stop in Castelo de Vide (p. 93) before arrival in Marvão (p. 92). *Pousada de Santa Maria.*

Day 15, Marvão to Trujillo (179 km). Return to N-118 (N-521 in Spain) and drive east through Cáceres to Trujillo (p. 145). If you had an early start, you might want to turn north at Membrio and go 31 km to Alcántara for a look at the Roman bridge, then south on 523 through Cáceres to Trujillo. This will add more kilometers but not too many if you love Roman ruins. *Parador Nacional de Trujillo.*

Day 16, Trujillo to Jarandilla de la Vera (107 km directly, 190 km via Guadalupe). Either go directly to Jarandilla (N-V to Navalmoral de la Mata, and then north 33 km to Jarandilla) or visit Guadalupe en route. Leave Trujillo heading south on C-524. Drive northeast at Zorita on C-401 to Guadalupe (p. 139). Leave Guadalupe heading north through Navalmoral de la Mata to Jarandilla (p. 140). *Parador Nacional Carlos V.*

Day 17, Jarandilla de la Vera to Madrid (212 km). Return to Navalmoral de la Mata then head east on N-V. You may want to stop in Lagartera (p. 86) and Oropesa (p. 85) or purchase pottery in Talavera before continuing to Madrid (p. 81).

NOTE: Page numbers following Spanish locales refer to *Paradores of Spain;* page numbers following Portuguese locales refer to *Pousadas of Portugal.*

Days 18 and 19, Madrid.

Day 20, Madrid to Toledo (70 km). Early start southwest, to spend most of the day in Toledo (p. 89). *Parador Nacional Conde de Orgaz.*

Day 21, Toledo to Almagro (139 km). Leave Toledo south on N-401 to Ciudad Real, then go 23 km southeast to Almagro (p. 77). *Parador Nacional de Almagro.*

Day 22, Almagro to Ubeda (162 km). Easy drive south to Bailén, then east to Ubeda (p. 57). *Parador Nacional Condestable Dávalos.*

Day 23, Ubeda to Granada (173 km via Jaén). Drive southwest through Baeza for a stop in Jaén (p. 49) before continuing to Granada (p. 47). *Parador Nacional San Francisco.*

Day 24, Granada. Full day of sightseeing. *Parador Nacional San Francisco.*

179 km to Málaga. Take time to stop in Nerja (p. 54) en route.

52 days, Ballards' choice, Barcelona to Madrid or vice versa

Day 1, Barcelona to Aiguablava (155 km). Leave Barcelona heading northeast along the coast through many enchanting villages before arriving in Aiguablava (p. 123). Allow a full day for this drive for you will want to make several stops. *Parador Nacional Costa Brava.*

Day 2, Aiguablava. Visits to Pals and La Bisbal or a drive north to fishing village and artists' enclave of Cadaqués. *Parador Nacional Costa Brava.*

Day 3, Aiguablava to Cardona (220 km). Leave Aiguablava heading north through Bagur then west to Gerona for the *autopista* south. Exit at Martorell (or sign to Montserrat). Visit Montserrat before continuing north through Manresa to Cardona (p. 127). *Parador Nacional Duques de Cardona.*

Day 4, Cardona to Benicarló (300 km). Retrace yesterday's route and enter Barcelona-Valencia *autopista* at Martorell, south to Benicarló (p. 173). A lot of kilometers, but fast going on the *autopista*. Maybe even time for the wine museum at Vilafranca del Penedés (p. 133). *Parador Nacional Costa del Azáhar.*

Day 5, Benicarló to El Saler (136 km). Early start heading south on the *autopista* to El Saler (p. 174), where there is a golf course. *Parador Nacional Luis Vives.*

Day 6, El Saler to Alarcón (214 km). Leave El Saler through Valencia west on N-111 to Alarcón (p. 74). *Parador Nacional Marqués de Villena.*

NOTE: Page numbers following Spanish locales refer to *Paradores of Spain;* page numbers following Portuguese locales refer to *Pousadas of Portugal.*

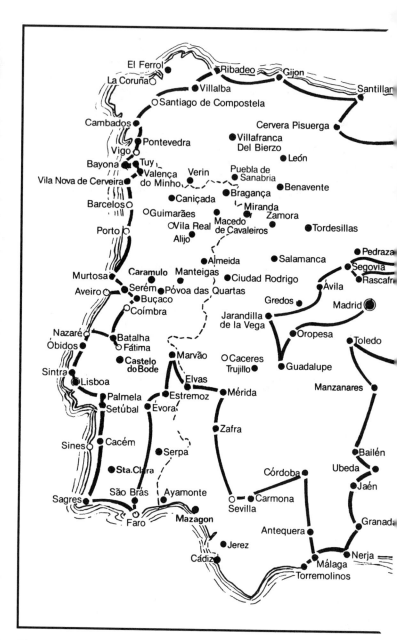

Itinerary 13

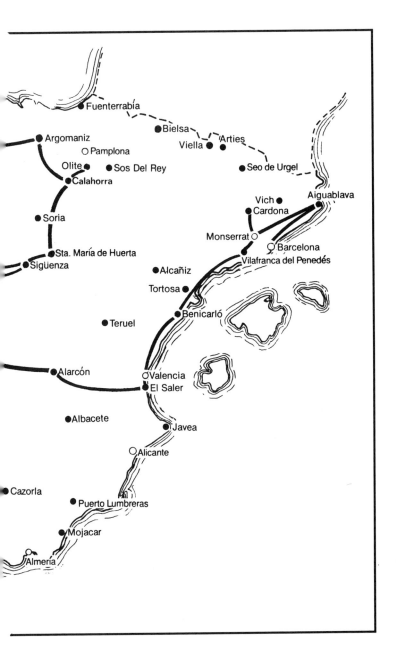

Day 7, Alarcón to Toledo (214 km). Drive northwest on N-111 to Tarancón, west through Aranjuez, south to Toledo (p. 89). *Parador Nacional Conde de Orgaz.*

Day 8, Toledo. Parador Nacional Conde de Orgaz.

Day 9, Toledo to Ubeda (268 km). Leave Toledo heading southeast on C-400 and pick up N-IV at Madridejos, south to Bailén (p. 38), east on N-322 to Ubeda (p. 57). *Parador Nacional Condestable Dávalos.*

Day 10, Ubeda to Granada (173 km via Jaén). Early start from Ubeda southwest through Baeza for stop in Jaén (p. 49) before continuing to Granada (p. 47). *Parador Nacional San Francisco.*

Day 11, Granada. Parador Nacional San Francisco.

Day 12, Granada to Torremolinos (195 km). Stop in Nerja (p. 54) before continuing through Málaga (p. 50) to Torremolinos (p. 59). *Parador Nacional del Golf.*

Days 13 and 14, Málaga. Lunch at the parador, drive to Ronda, Casares (p. 60), Mijas, or along the coast toward Gibraltar. *Parador Nacional del Golf.*

Day 15, Torremolinos to Córdoba (192 km). Back through Málaga, north through Antequera (p. 33) to Córdoba (p. 44). *Parador Nacional La Arruzafa.*

Day 16, Córdoba. Bus tour of the city or independent exploration. *Parador Nacional La Arruzafa.*

Day 17, Córdoba to Carmona (105 km). Early start from Córdoba to Carmona (p. 41). Check into parador then take bus into Sevilla for walking tour. *Parador Nacional Alcázar del Rey Don Pedro.*

Day 18, Carmona to Mérida (231 km). Another early start, heading back through Sevilla north to Zafra (p. 147) for a rest and perhaps lunch before going on to Mérida (p. 142). *Parador Nacional Via de la Plata.*

Day 19, Mérida and Roman ruins. Parador Nacional Via de la Plata.

Day 20, Mérida to Marvão (161 km). Leave Mérida heading east through Badajoz. Stop at pousada in Elvas (p. 96) before driving north on N-246 through Portalegre to Marvão (p. 92). *Pousada de Santa Maria.*

Day 21, Marvão to Estremoz (78 km). Retrace yesterday's route through Portalegre, then take N-18 to Estremoz (p. 98). Time en route for a visit to Vila Viçosa (p. 100). *Pousada da Rainha Santa Isabel.*

Day 22, Estremoz to Evora (61 km via Arraiolos). Drive east from Estremoz on N-4 to Arraiolos. Even if not interested in buying, do take time to visit the shops to see the beautiful locally made

---

NOTE: Page numbers following Spanish locales refer to *Paradores of Spain;* page numbers following Portuguese locales refer to *Pousadas of Portugal.*

carpets before continuing southeast to Evora (p. 102). *Pousada dos Lóios.*

Day 23, Evora. Pousada dos Lóios.

Day 24, Evora to São Brás de Alportel (199 km). Drive south, possibly stopping in Beja (p. 107), then over to N-2 and south to São Brás de Alportel (p. 107). *Pousada de São Brás de Alportel.*

Day 25, São Brás de Alportel to Sagres (141 km). Early start from São Brás to allow stops in Faro, or any of many coastal villages. Good shopping in Albufeira and Lagos. *Pousada do Infante.*

Day 26, Sagres and environs. Pousada do Infante.

Day 27, Sagres to Setúbal or Palmela (216 km). Drive north on N-120 for a stop in Santiago do Cacém for 1 P.M. lunch then on to Setúbal or Palmela. *Pousada de São Filipe or Pousada do Castelo de Palmela.*

Day 28, Setúbal, Troia Peninsula, Azeitão. Pousada de São Filipe or Pousada do Castelo de Palmela.

Day 29, Setúbal to Lisboa (50 km). Majority of day in Lisboa.

Days 30, 31, and 32, Lisboa (p. 28).

Day 33, Lisboa to Sintra (30 km). Take the coastal route to Sintra (p. 35). Hotel Palácio dos Seteais.

Day 34, Sintra to Batalha (167 km). Early start from Sintra north for visits to Mafra (p. 39), Obidos (p. 41), Alcobaça (p. 45), and lunch at seaside cafe in Nazaré (p. 43). *Late arrival* in Batalha (p. 47). *Pousada do Mestre Afonso Domingues.*

Day 35, Batalha and environs. Trips to Fátima (p. 49) and Tomar (p. 51). *Pousada do Mestre Afonso Domingues.*

Day 36, Batalha to Buçaco (110 km). Drive north through Leiria on N-1 for short stop in Conímbriga (p. 53). Try to allow at least three hours in Coimbra (p. 53) before continuing 32 km northeast through Luso to Buçaco (p. 56). *Palace Hotel.*

Day 37, Buçaco to Murtosa (111 km). Enjoy early morning walk in Buçaco forest before driving back through Luso to N-1, north to Santo António Agueda (you might want to stop in Serém at gracious Pousada de Santo António [p. 61] for a cup of coffee), west to Aveiro for a visit of two or three hours. Leave Aveiro (p. 64) to Angeja, north to Estarreja, southwest to Murtosa (p. 63). *Pousada da Ria.*

Day 38, Murtosa to Valença do Minho or Vila Nova de Cerveira (237 km/225 km via Barcelos, 200 km/188 km via Porto). If it's Thursday, enjoy market day in Barcelos (p. 68). If not, you may choose to spend several hours in Porto (p. 65). In any case, leave Murtosa and head back through Estarreja, north to Ovar, and east to

NOTE: Page numbers following Spanish locales refer to *Paradores of Spain;* page numbers following Portuguese locales refer to *Pousadas of Portugal.*

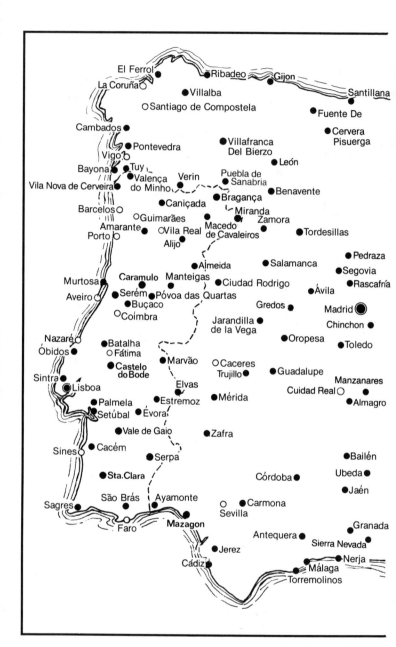

Your choice

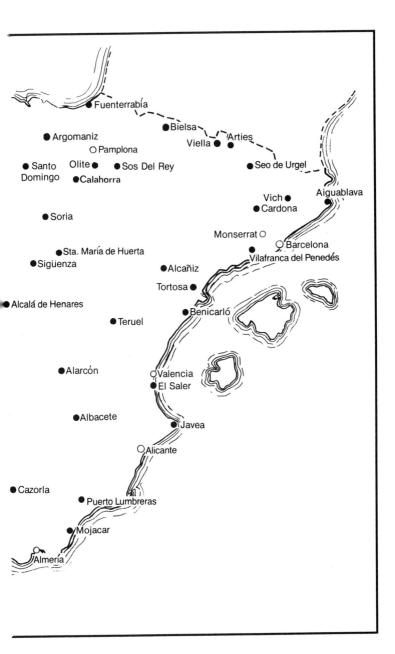

Highway N-1. From either Porto or Barcelos, travel scenic N-13 along the coast to Valença do Minho (p. 75) or Vila Nova de Cerveira (p. 73). *Pousada de São Teotónio or Pousada de Dom Dinis.*

Day 39, Valença do Minho to Bayona (60 km). Enjoy shopping in the morning in Valença. Cross the international bridge into Spain and Tuy (p. 162). From Tuy, drive southwest to Laguardia and north to Bayona (p. 152). *Parador Nacional Conde de Gondomar.*

Day 40, Bayona to Santiago de Compostela (113 km). Leave Bayona and go northeast through Vigo, Pontevedra (p. 157), west through Sanjenjo, north to Cambados (p. 154) for a visit and rest. Retrace a few kilometers and then cut east and north on C-550 to Santiago de Compostela (p. 159). *Hotel Reyes Católicos.*

Day 41, Santiago to Ribadeo (147 km). Drive northeast from Santiago de Compostela on C-544 and then pick up N-VI and at Bahamond turn northeast on N-634 for lunch at the parador in Villalba (p. 165). Take N-634 again north to Ribadeo (p. 158). *Parador Nacional de Ribadeo.*

Day 42, Ribadeo to Gijón (211 km). Take the coastal route and at Avilés turn north to Cabo Peñas and down to Luanco and into Gijón (p. 70). *Parador Nacional Molino Viejo.*

Day 43, Gijón to Santillana del Mar (193 km). Leave Gijón heading south on C-630 to Noreña, east on N-634 past San Vicente de la Banquera, then C-6316 to Santillana (p. 110). Go at once to the reception center at the caves of Altamira and put your name on the list for possible entry to the caves. *Parador Nacional Gil Blas.*

Day 44, Santillana del Mar to Cervera de Pisuerga (112 km). Drive east a few kilometers to pick up N-611 south to Aguilar de Campóo, then west 25 km to Cervera de Pisuerga (p. 97). *Parador Nacional Fuentes Carrionas.*

Day 45, Cervera to Argómaniz (267 km via Burgos). Retrace the 25 km to Aguilar de Campóo, then south to Burgos if you wish. Otherwise go from Aguilar to La Nuez de Arriba and east on N-232 all the way to Vitoria and Argómaniz (p. 181). *Parador Nacional de Argómaniz.*

Day 46, Argómaniz to Olite (144 km or 155 km if via Calahorra). Drive south through the rich Rioja wine country. Wine tasting at bodegas in Laguardia. Follow the secondary road north of the Ebro River. You might have lunch at the parador in Calahorra (p. 96) before turning north to Olite (p. 169). *Parador Nacional Príncipe de Viana.*

Day 47, Olite to Sigüenza (259 km). Get on the Zaragoza *autopista* at Tafalla. Exit at signs to Soria (p. 115), take N-111 south to Medinaceli (p. 109), and go west to Sigüenza (p. 87). *Parador Nacional Castillo de Sigüenza.*

Note: Page numbers following Spanish locales refer to *Paradores of Spain;* page numbers following Portuguese locales refer to *Pousadas of Portugal.*

Day 48, Sigüenza to Segovia (236 km). Leave Sigüenza south on C-204, then pick up E-4. If you wish to avoid Madrid, take the airport freeway north past the airport, through Alcobendas, across N-1 to C-601, north and west through Navacerrada, and north on N-601 to Segovia (p. 113). *Parador Nacional de Segovia.*

Day 49, Segovia to Avila (65 km). Morning in Segovia, rest of day in Avila (p. 93). *Parador Nacional Raimundo de Borgoña.*

Day 50, Avila to Jarandilla de la Vera (144 km). Mountain roads as you cross the Sierra de Gredos. Leave Avila heading south on C-502. At Arenas de San Pedro turn west to Jarandilla de la Vera (p. 140). *Parador Nacional Carlos V.*

Day 51, Jarandilla de la Vera to Guadalupe (77 km). South through Navalmoral de la Mata to Guadalupe (p. 139). *Parador Nacional Zurbarán.*

Day 52, Guadalupe to Oropesa (91 km). Drive south then east through Puerto de San Vicente and north to Oropesa (p. 85). Plenty of time to shop in Lagartera. *Parador Nacional Virrey Toledo.*

148 km to Madrid.

PRONUNCIATION GUIDE

Alcácer do Sal: *al-CAH-sair doo SAHL*
Alijó: *ah-lee-ZHOO*
Almeida: *al-MAY-duh*
Amarante: *ah-muh-RAHNT*
Batalha: *buh-TIE-yuh*
Bragança: *bruh-GAHN-suh*
Buçaco: *boo-SAH-coo*
Caniçada: *cahn-ee-SAH-duh*
Caramulo: *car-uh-MOO-loo*
Cascais: *cush-CAISH*
Castelo do Bode: *cas-TELL-oo doo BOD* (long o)
Elvas: *ELL-vahss*
Estremoz: *esh-truh-MOSH*
Evora: *AY-vo-ruh*
Fátima: *FAH-tee-mah*
Gondarem: *gon-DAR-ain*
Guimarães: *gee-muh-RYE-aish* (hard g)
Lisboa: *liz-BOH-uh*
Macedo de Cavaleiros: *mah-SAY-doh day cah-vah-LYAY-rosh*
Manteigas: *mahn-TAY-gus*
Marvão: *mar-VOWN*
Miranda do Douro: *mih-RAN-duh doo DOH-roh*
Monção: *mohn-SOWN*
Murtosa: *mur-TOE-suh*
Obidos: *OH-bee-dosh*
Palmela: *paul-MELL-uh*
Penha: *PAIN-yuh*
Ponte de Lima: *POHNT duh LEE-muh*
Póvoa das Quartas: *POH-voh-uh dahss KWART-ahss*
Queluz: *kay-LOOSH*
Sagres: *SAH-gruss*
Sangalhos: *sawn-GUY-yose*
Santa Clara-a-Velha: *SAWN-tuh CLAIR-uh ah VAY-yuh*
Santiago do Cacém: *sawn-tee-AH-goo doo kah-SAYM*
São Brás de Alportel: *sown BRAHSS day al-por-TELL*
Serém: *suh-RAYM*
Serpa: *SAIR-pah*
Setúbal: *SHTEW-bal*
Sintra: *SEEN-trah*
Valença do Minho: *vah-LEN-suh doo MEEN-you*
Viana do Castelo: *vee-AHN-uh doo cahs-TELL-oh*
Vila Nova de Cerveira: *vil-luh NO-vuh day sair-VAY-ruh*

GLOSSARY

ADEGA. A wine cellar or winery.

ALB. A long white robe worn by a priest during mass.

ALMOHADS. Muslims who arrived in Portugal in 1146.

ALMORAVIDS. Muslims from North Africa who reached the Algarve in 1086.

APSE. Vaulted semicircular recess in church at end of choir.

ARCHIVOLT. Decorative band around an arch.

ARMILLARY SPHERE. Ancient astronomical instrument made up of rings representing positions of important circles of the celestial sphere; turns on its polar axis and has a meridian and horizon.

ARTESONADO. Coffered wooden ceiling.

ASTROLABE. Instrument developed after the armillary sphere for viewing positions of celestial bodies.

AUTO-DA-FÉ. Literally "act of faith"; ceremony following sentence by Inquisition and preceding execution of that sentence; also, burning of one condemned as a heretic.

AZULEJOS. Tiles, originally glazed blue (*azul*), first made in 1565.

BAROQUE. Extravagant decoration used from 1600 to 1750.

BYZANTINE. In architecture, buildings of masonry, with round arches, low domes; use of frescoes and mosaics; period after 476.

CHALICE. Cup for wine of eucharist or mass.

CHANCEL. Space around altar, usually enclosed, used by clergy.

CHASUBLE. Sleeveless, outer vestment worn by priest during mass.

CHOIR. Part of cruciform church east of the crossing.

CISTERCIAN. Member of an order of monks and nuns founded in 1098 in France, under rule of Saint Benedict.

CITÂNIA. Settlement of prehistoric hill tribes.

CLOISTER. Covered walkway of arcades opening onto a courtyard.

CORBEL. A bracket projecting from a wall to support an arch.

DISCALCED. Pertaining to religious orders whose members go shoeless or wear sandals.

ESPIGUEIRO. Family granary similar to Spain's *horreo*; built of vertical wooden slats, roofed with slate, topped with granite cross, elevated on pillars to discourage rodents.

FLEMISH. Pertaining to Flanders, medieval country in western Europe that encompassed the modern regions of western Belgium and adjacent parts of southwestern Netherlands and northern France.

FORAL. Charter awarded to village or settlement by king.

GOTHIC. Architecture originating in France in the mid-1100s; marked by pointed arches, ribbed vaults, fine wood and stone work, use of flying buttresses and ornamental gables.

HIERONYMITE. Member of a hermit order named in honor of Saint Jerome.

INFANTA. Daughter of a king, not heir to throne; wife of Infante.

INFANTE. Son of a king, not heir to throne.

INQUISITION. Religious court or tribunal under royal control, set up to ferret out those thought to be heretics.

JOANINE. Style of architecture and decoration used during the reign of João V (1706-50). It was moderately Baroque, with white-washed exteriors, ornate granite-trimmed interiors (examples: monastery at Mafra, library of University of Coimbra, and aqueduct of Lisbon).

JUDIARIA. A designated area where Jews were forced to live during Moorish occupation, continuing through Inquisition days.

LARGO. Small square.

MANUELINE. Transitional architectural style (from Gothic to Renaissance) peculiar to Portugal during the reign of Manoel I (1495-1521), lasting through first quarter of the sixteenth century; dramatic use of sea subjects; twisted forms in columns, ribs, corbels; delicate, intricate stucco tracery (examples: Monastery of Batalha, Monastery of Belém, and Convent of Christ in Tomar); Boytac was leading proponent.

MEDIEVAL. Pertaining to the Middle Ages.

MERLON. Solid part between two open spaces on a battlement.

MIDDLE AGES. From the late fifth century to around 1350.

MONSTRANCE. Receptacle in which consecrated host (bread or wafer regarded as body of Christ in the mass) is exposed for adoration.

MORISCO. Christianized Moor.

MOURARIA. Designated area where Moors were forced to live after the Reconquest.

MOZARAB. Christian living under Moorish rule.

MUDEJAR. Christianized Moor; in architecture, style characterized by key-shaped arches, decorative ceiling panels, and intricate open work on chimneys.

ORDER OF THE GARTER. Oldest and most illustrious British order of knighthood, established by Edward III in 1348.

ORDER OF THE GOLDEN FLEECE. Chivalric order founded in 1430 in Bruges, Flanders, by Philip the Good, duke of Burgundy, to celebrate his wedding to Princess Isabella of Portugal (daughter of João I, sister of Prince Henry the Navigator).

PELOURINHO. Town pillory sometimes used for hanging criminals; at other times, errant was chained to rings at the top of the structure.

POLYPTYCH. Four or more panels of paintings hinged and folding together, sometimes used as altarpiece.

POMBALINE. Style of architecture used during rebuilding of Lisboa after the earthquake, when Pombal was prime minister.

PRAÇA. Large square.

PRAIA. Beach.

QUINTA. Country estate.

RECONQUEST. Period in Portugal and Spain having to do with reconquering territory held by Moors.

REFECTORY. Dining hall of religious building.

RENAISSANCE. Period beginning in fourteenth century, continuing until the seventeenth.

RETABLE. Ornamental structure above and in back of an altar.

ROMANESQUE. In architecture, period from the ninth through twelfth centuries; heavy masonry construction with narrow openings; round arches; groin and barrel vaults.

ROMARIA. Religious festival in honor of a patron saint followed by secular celebrations.

SACRISTY. Room in the church where sacred vessels and vestments are stored.

SÉ. Center of authority or jurisdiction of a bishop; a cathedral.

TEMPLAR. Member of religious-military order founded by crusaders in Jerusalem about 1118.

TORRE DE MENAGEM. The keep or strongest part of a castle.

TRIPTYCH. Set of three connected panels bearing pictures, sometimes used as an altarpiece.

VISIGOTH. Western division of Goths (Germanic tribes), who formed monarchy in Iberia about 500 and maintained it until 711. Visigothic architecture characterized by rough-hewn stones without mortar; carved friezes of geometric or scroll motifs and Christian symbols; horseshoe arches.

INDEX BY LOCALE

INDEX
BY ESTABLISHMENT

SUBJECT INDEX

HARVARD COMMON PRESS books are available at bookstores or from the Harvard Common Press, 535 Albany Street, Boston, Massachusetts 02118. When ordering from the publisher, include $2 postage and handling; if you live in Massachusetts, also include 5 percent sales tax.

Other travel books published by the Harvard Common Press are listed below. A complete catalog of books is available on request.

PARADORES OF SPAIN: UNIQUE LODGINGS IN STATE-OWNED CASTLES, CONVENTS, MANSIONS, AND HOTELS
By Sam and Jane Ballard
$8.95 paper, ISBN 0-916782-76-X
256 pages

A companion volume to *Pousadas of Portugal*, this is the only published guide to the luxurious lodgings owned and operated by the Spanish government. The Ballards, who have visited every parador, provide detailed maps, photographs, and suggested itineraries as well as lively descriptions of the accommodations and their historic settings.

BEST PLACES TO STAY IN AMERICA'S CITIES: UNIQUE HOTELS, CITY INNS, AND BED AND BREAKFASTS
Edited by Kenneth Hale
$9.95 paper, ISBN 0-916782-84-0
346 pages

For travelers seeking the charm and personal service of small lodging places, this book describes the best hotels, inns, and B&Bs in the fifty most visited cities in the United States. *Available October 1986.*

BEST PLACES TO STAY IN NEW ENGLAND
By Christina Tree and Bruce Shaw
$9.95 paper, ISBN 0-916782-74-3
364 pages

A guide to the best accommodations in New England—including inns, small hotels, motels, resorts, B&Bs, and farms—grouped according to the kind of vacation experience offered.

HOW TO TAKE GREAT TRIPS WITH YOUR KIDS
By Sanford and Joan Portnoy
$14.95 cloth, ISBN 0-916782-52-5
$8.95 paper, ISBN 0-916782-51-4
192 pages

Traveling with the kids can be fun and easy, once you know some special techniques. Whether you're driving to Aunt Helen's or flying to Zanzibar, this book offers the ABCs of planning, packing, and en-route problem solving.

THE PORTABLE PET: HOW TO TRAVEL ANYWHERE WITH YOUR DOG OR CAT
By Barbara Nicholas
$12.95 cloth, ISBN 0-916782-50-6
$5.95 paper, ISBN 0-916782-49-2
96 pages

If vacation wouldn't be the same without your faithful friend, or you're planning to move your pet along with the rest of your household, you're headed into a maze of requirements and regulations. Find the answers to all your questions in this lively and pragmatic guide.

EXPLORING OUR NATIONAL PARKS AND MONUMENTS
Revised Eighth Edition
By Devereux Butcher
$10.95 paper, ISBN 0-87645-122-9
400 pages

"This is very possibly the best available collection of photographs of our national parks. Schools and libraries will find it an admirable guide and sourcebook as will the traveler."—*Library Journal*

A TRAVELER'S GUIDE TO THE SMOKY MOUNTAINS REGION
By Jeff Bradley
$19.95 cloth, ISBN 0-916782-63-8
$10.95 paper, ISBN 0-916782-64-6
288 pages

The first comprehensive and critical guide to southern Appalachia, a land of outstanding natural beauty and old-time graciousness.

"A thoroughgoing, level-headed guide through some fascinating hills!"—*Roy Blount, Jr.*

INSIDE OUTLETS: THE BEST BARGAIN SHOPPING IN NEW ENGLAND
By Naomi R. Rosenberg and Marianne W. Sekulow
$8.95 paper, ISBN 0-916782-66-2
224 pages

A critical, quality-conscious guide to the best of New England's bargain shops. Special features include price-quality ratings, shopping "itineraries" in scenic areas, and over $100 worth of money-saving coupons from New England merchants.

THE BEST THINGS IN NEW YORK ARE FREE
By Marian Hamilton
$10.95 paper, ISBN 0-916782-75-1
560 pages

A comprehensive guide to every free attraction in New York City, including museums and historic houses, art galleries, films and concerts, tours, libraries, parks, and cultural societies. Over a thousand listings.

THE CAREFREE GETAWAY GUIDE FOR NEW YORKERS
By Theodore Scull
$8.95 paper, ISBN 0-916782-68-9
208 pages

For restless New Yorkers, Scull describes forty day and weekend trips in New York and its environs, including Connecticut, Pennsylvania, Rhode Island, and New Jersey. All trips are by safe, convenient public transportation, and detailed maps are provided.